MATH PIRATES

THE COMPLETE QUEST FOR THE PICKLED PEARL

MATH PIRATES

THE COMPLETE QUEST FOR THE PICKLED PEARL

S.E. BURR

E.M.
TIPPETTS
BOOK DESIGNS

TABLE OF CONTENTS

MATH PIRATES

THE SEARCH FOR PIRATE PETE

BOOK 1: COLLECTING & ANALYZING DATA

S.E. BURR

THE SEARCH FOR PIRATE PETE

"**C**ome in, my boy! Come in!" says Grandpa Pirate, the most fearsome pirate in all the seven seas.

You walk into Grandpa Pirate's parlor where he sits sipping tea, his pinky finger in the air. "Sit, my boy! Sit!"

So you take a seat across from him, and he pours you a cup of tea, which you sip, pinky finger raised, just like proper pirates do it. "Yum," you say, "that's some tasty tea."

"Yum," he agrees. "Now I bet you wonder why I brought you here."

"Yes, sir," you say.

"As you know, I'm the most fearsome pirate in all of Pirate Town," he says.

"And in all the seven seas!" you answer.

He laughs. "Perhaps, perhaps, I, Grandpa Pirate, the most fearsome pirate in all of Pirate Town and perhaps the seven seas, too, am planning to put up my pirate hat and retire to live on the land as a regular old landlubber. My period of piracy is past."

"No!" you exclaim.

"Yes!" he answers.

"Never!" you say.

"Now!" he answers, "and I'm looking for a worthy person to take my place as captain of my pirate ship, the infamous, Pickled Pearl."

"You are?" you ask.

"I am," he answers, "and I think you might be just the person for the job. Are you prepared for such a promotion?"

"Me?" you ask.

"You," he answers.

"Well..." you say.

"What?" he asks.

"Probably..." you say.

"Probably?" he asks.

"Well, no, not probably," you say. "I've only ever been a cabin boy, so probably not probably, but possibly."

"Possibly?" he asks.

"Possibly I'm prepared," you say. "It's possible I am, and I thank you for the opportunity."

Then Grandpa Pirate laughs out loud, a

huge guffaw, spraying the room and everything in it, you included, with tea. "Possibly!" he says, "possibly! Well, I appreciate your honesty, but you're not prepared! No way!"

"I'm not?" you ask.

"Not by a mile," he says. "You're leagues away from being ready."

"Oh," you say, your head dropping to stare at your toes dangling from the chair.

"Don't look so disappointed," says Grandpa Pirate. "I have a quest for you to practice piracy. If you complete it, you will be prepared to become captain of my prestigious pirate vessel, the Pickled Pearl."

"Oh!" you say and smile. "What do I have to do?"

He hands you a piece of paper and a pencil. "Do you know what this is?"

As you unfold the paper, you quickly

realize it's a map. Could it be a map to a buried treasure?

No, it isn't.

"This is a map of Pirate Town," you say.

"Yes, my boy! Yes! And somewhere in Pirate Town is Pirate Pete, my first mate. He has an eyepatch on his right eye, a brown beard, and gray striped pants. Find him and he'll give you another map. Guess what that one will be!"

"Pirate Village?" you ask.

"Har har har," he laughs. "Arr, no. That one will be a treasure map. Once you have the map, come back and speak to me and I'll tell you about the next step in your quest."

"Okay," you say, jumping to your feet, but then you hesitate. "How do I find Pirate Pete?"

"That's the question, isn't it? You'll have to figure it out. That's the first part of your pirate practice."

"Okay," you say. "Thank you, Grandpa Pirate. I'll see you soon."

"See you soon," he answers and pours himself more tea.

The first thing you think to do is go visit your friend Marina. She's a mermaid and the smartest person (or merson) you know, but as you leave Grandpa Pirate's house someone speaks to you from the bushes.

"Psst, kid!" they say. You look in that direction and all you see is a patchy looking parrot perched on a peony.

You take a few cautious steps toward the bird and see a head peak over the bush. It's a pirate. He gestures for you to come closer.

You take a couple steps closer.

"Is that a map?" asks the pirate.

"Maybe," you say, holding the folded paper tighter.

"I'll buy it from you," the pirate says and holds up a pouch. As he does, you hear coins jingle together inside. "Five genuine gold doubloons for your map."

He thinks it's a treasure map, but it's not. It's just a map of Pirate Town, and you don't think you need a map of Pirate Town. You've lived in Pirate Town forever and know it like the back of your hand.

Do you:

Sell the map Grandpa Pirate gave you

(turn to page 9)?

or

Keep the map Grandpa Pirate gave you

(turn to page 18)?

You're back outside Grandpa Pirate's house, and Percival the Pirate has just offered to buy the map of Pirate Town from you. This time you're going to make a different choice and sell him the map.

SELL THE MAP

You know your way around Pirate Town so well that you don't think you need a map, and besides pirates have to be flexible, which means ready to change their plans if things don't go the way they expect. You certainly didn't expect to meet this pirate hiding in the bushes right outside Grandpa Pirate's house. Also, all pirates love gold.

Maybe this is actually part of Grandpa Pirate's piracy practice. Maybe Grandpa Pirate asked this pirate to offer to buy the map from you to see if you would get the gold or you would hold on to a useless map for no reason.

"Sure," you say. "You toss me the gold and I'll toss you the map." You know better than to get too close to a strange pirate. If you did, he might just snatch the map from you and run off without giving you the money.

"Okay," he says. "On three—one, two, three."

He throws the sack of coins and you throw the map. You catch the coins. The parrot takes off from the peony bush and snatches the map from the air. Then both the pirate and the bird take off, the pirate running down the street, and the parrot flying above him.

Why were they so eager to get away?

As quick as you can, you open the bag and look at the coins. They're not gold at all! Nothing but tin. You chase after the pirate as he runs between buildings, down back alleys, and takes a twisting path across Pirate Town. The parrot makes him easier to follow because it flies above him, and even when you lose sight of the pirate, you can still see the bird's bright red feathers.

But then the bird swoops down and you can no longer see it. You run to the place you think it landed but don't find it there. You're in a dead-end alley. There is a group of mangy cats feasting on fish scraps in the alley, but no pirate and no parrot. The air smells of garbage and fish, so you can't tell by the pirate's powerful odor whether he came this way. Two doors leave the alleyway, one to the left and one to the right. You think the pirate and parrot must have gone through one of them, but have no way to know which.

You stop and listen. It's been a long chase, and it's hard to catch your breath. You hear the cats enjoying their lunch, the cries of seagulls, and the sounds of waves. You've come quite near to the shore. Then you hear a crash through the closed door to your right, and an angry shopkeeper says, "Grab hold of your squawker, scalawag! You break it, you buy it!"

Rushing through the right-hand door, you see that the shop woman has grabbed hold of the pirate by the beard and is swatting him with a rolled newspaper. The excited parrot is circling around the room above their heads. In a mess on the floor are a number of prosthetics.

Everyone's heard about how pirates might have a hook instead of a hand or a peg leg instead of a leg and foot, but those are just two of many piratical replacements. Instead of a hook, a pirate can get a carved hand, a knife or sword for fighting, a fork for eating, or even a spyglass for looking. There aren't many alternatives to a peg leg, except for a fully carved foot, but peg legs come in a variety of styles and materials, beautifully polished or painted, some even jewel encrusted. The parrot had knocked several to the floor. If the pirate were a gentleman, he would stop and help the shopkeeper clean up the mess.

Yeah, right! As soon as he sees you, the pirate yanks himself free from the shopkeeper's grasp with a yell. Several strands of the pirate's beard remain clutched in the woman's hand as the pirate's quick escape pulls them clear out of his face. "Pamela, to me!" he shouts as he flees out the back

The parrot responds instantly, swooping

to follow.

You're hot on their trail, but the shop woman grabs hold of the back of your shirt. "Where do you think you're going, rascal?"

"That man stole my map!" you answer.

"Percival the Pirate is a real ruffian," she says. "He'll take more from you than that if you keep chasing him. Besides, someone's got to help me clean up this mess."

"But I didn't knock this stuff over!" you say.

"Oh, is that right? And would this stuff have been knocked over if you hadn't chased that scalawag and his squawker in here?"

No, it wouldn't have, so you have to stop and help her clean up. When you finally make it out of the back of the shop, all you see is a beach empty but for seagulls and seals. You've lost them!

Percival the Pirate and Pamela the Parrot have gotten away with the map Grandpa Pirate gave you. What would Grandpa Pirate say if he saw you now? You hang your head in shame. You've gone completely across Pirate Town. You're nowhere near Marina the Mermaid's cove now and don't think you have time to ask her for advice. At least, you still have the pencil Grandpa Pirate gave you and the pouch of nearly worthless tin. You walk back into the shop with the pouch and pencil in your hands.

"Hey, what's in that pouch?" the shopkeeper asks you.

You show her.

"Tin, huh?" She laughs. "Percival cheated you with one of the oldest tricks in the book, didn't he?"

You nod, sadly.

She frowns. "Oh, buck up, lad. Hey,

I could use that tin in my prosthetics. I have some paper here I'll trade you for it."

You know it's a good deal. Paper is difficult to make and expensive. You nod. "Thank you," you say, taking the paper and handing over the tin.

Now what will you do? You know Pirate Town well. You're confident that you can draw a new map, though it'll take you some time. You've already been delayed in finding Pirate Pete.

Do you take more time to draw a new map
(turn to page 26)?

or

Do you take off right now to go find him
(turn to page 37)?

You're back outside Grandpa Pirate's house and Percival the Pirate has just offered to buy the map of Pirate Town from you. This time you're going to make a different choice and keep the map.

KEEP THE MAP

You don't know why Grandpa Pirate gave you a map of Pirate Town, but he must have had a good reason. Besides, it's not smart to do business with strange pirates. The pirate probably would have tried to cheat you somehow. Maybe the coins he offered you were fake. "No thanks," you say. "I'm keeping the map."

"Get the map, Pamela!" the pirate yells, and the parrot takes off from the peony bush and flies at you, swooping to snatch the map from your hand, but you stuff it into your pocket and take off running.

The parrot and pirate chase after you.

You weave between streets and alleys, heading toward the cove where Marina lives. You lose them and make it there safely.

You show Marina the map and tell her what Grandpa Pirate told you.

"Oh yeah," she says, "Pirate Pete, I know him—eye patch, beard, striped pants."

"You do?" you ask. "That's great! Where is he?"

"I don't know," she answers. "I haven't seen him in a while."

"Oh," you say, head hanging.

"Do you know your way around Pirate

Town?" Marina asks.

"Of course," you say. "I know it like the back of my hand."

"So why do you think Grandpa Pirate gave you a map?"

"Huh," you say. "So I won't get lost?"

"But you wouldn't get lost, would you?" she asks. "Not since you know Pirate Town so well."

"Probably not," you answer.

"Did he give you anything else?" she asks.

"No," you say, but then you remember and pull the pencil from your pocket. "Yes, he gave me this."

Marina puts her finger on her chin and wrinkles her forehead in her thinking face. "A map and a pencil. So, maybe he plans for you to write on the map. What would you write on a map?"

"The path I plan to take?" you say. That's the only thing you've ever seen anyone draw on a map.

"Possibly," says Marina.

"Possibly?" you ask.

She nods. "Possibly, but probably not. I can think of a good way this map might help you find Pirate Pete. You can do a survey."

"A what?" you ask.

"A survey is where you ask many people the same questions and record their answers," she said. "What you can do is go around town and ask people if they've seen Pete and ask them to mark where they saw him on the map."

"Oh! Good idea!" you exclaim, but then you hesitate, "but what if they don't know Pete?"

"Hmm, good point," says Marina.

You think of another problem. "Do I

want a bunch of people to know I'm looking for Pirate Pete? Pirates aren't particularly trustworthy. In fact, a sneaky pirate chased me half the way here. If people know I'm looking for Pete, they may try to find him first and take the map from him."

"Pirate Pete is an excellent swordsman," says Marina. "If anyone tries to take the map, he can probably fight them off."

"Maybe," you say, "but no matter how good someone is with a sword, they can still be taken by surprise, and a sneaky pirate might not try to get it through fighting. He might try to pick Pete's pocket and take it without Pete noticing."

"True," agrees Marina. "Well, it seems to me you have two choices for how to do your survey. You can be specific or you can be vague."

"Tell me more," you say.

"If you're specific," says Marina, "you'll ask people if they've seen Pirate Pete. If they don't know Pirate Pete, you'll give them a description with specific details: He's Grandpa Pirate's first mate on the Pickled Pearl. He has an eyepatch on his right eye, a brown beard, and gray striped pants. That description is specific enough so that if people say they've seen him, it's probably him they've seen and not someone else. This is the faster way to find him because you won't be chasing after false leads, people who just look a bit like Pete. However, people will know you're looking for him, and like you said, they might try to take the map from him before you get there."

You nod.

Marina goes on. "The other choice is to be vague. You won't use Pete's name. You'll just ask people if they've seen a pirate with an eye patch, a beard, and striped pants. This method will probably be slower, because people will tell you they've seen him, when they've really seen someone else who looks like him. However, no one will know exactly who you're looking for, so they'll be less likely to get to him first."

Will you ask people specifically if they've seen Pirate Pete (turn to page 42)?

or

Will you be vague (turn to page 51)?

You're back at the Pirate Prosthetics Shop. You have paper that the Shopkeeper has given you in exchange for the tin you got from Percival the Pirate. This time you're going to make a different choice and redraw the map.

REDRAW THE MAP

You decide to redraw the map. Taking the time to draw the map will delay your search for Pirate Pete, but you think it'll be worth it in the end.

The shopkeeper lets you sit at her table to draw and gives you tea and crumpets to eat while you work. She turned out to be rather a nice lady after you helped her clean up the mess that that awful Percival Pirate left.

You know Pirate Town very well and you're good at drawing, so making a new map is not too difficult. Having a good snack helps you think, and while you work, you ponder why Grandpa Pirate gave you a map of town in the first place. You decide that having a map will help you keep track of the places you've already looked for Pirate Pete. You'll mark each place with an X after you've checked it.

Then you think about where you should look first. You don't know much about Pete, but you know plenty of pirates, and you think all pirates love three things: gold, singing pirate songs, and pets. You know where to find pirate songs and pets, but what about gold?

The bank?

Hah! Not in Pirate Town!

People would have to be mad to keep a

bunch of gold together in one place with pirates around! No, you won't be able to find him at a place with lots of gold, so you think of a fourth thing pirates like, tattoos.

When the map is finished, you ask the shopkeeper to look at it, and she points out a few things you got wrong. You quickly erase and redraw those parts, and it's good to go. You thank the shopkeeper and head out.

First, you go to the Sea Shanty Singalong. You squeeze into the back of the room. The place is packed with singing pirates. One man with a fine tenor sings out the verse:

As I was going to Derby, upon a
market day, I met with the finest
ram, sir, that ever was fed upon
hay.

Then everyone else sings back with the chorus:

That's a lie, that's a lie, that's a lie,
lie, lie.

You look around the room for Pirate Pete, but it's crowded and hard to see everyone. The main singer sings,

Now this is a wonderful old
ram, sir, was playful as a kid. He
swallowed the captain's spyglass
along with the bosuns fid.

As you keep looking, you join in with the chorus:

That's a lie, that's a lie, that's a lie,
lie, lie.

You see one guy with an eyepatch, but his beard is gray, not brown. Pirate Pete isn't here. As you leave, you hear the singer starting another verse:

> *One morning on the poop, sir,*
> *before eight bells was rung...*

The door swings closed behind you, cutting off the sound.

Next, you go to Pirate Pet Pavilion. Parrots are a well-known pirate pet and there are several of them in the shop, but lots of other critters are also for sale. There are monkeys, iguanas, geckos, parakeets and cats. Cats are handy to have on pirate ships because they chase rats which can cause disease and eat the food stores. Some of the cats are special. They have extra toes on their paws. This makes them excellent climbers. They can climb all over a ship and up into the rigging, no problem, and they're really cute, too. You scratch one under the chin.

There are several pirates in the shop. One has a brown mustache, but no beard, and the eye patch is on his left rather than his right eye. Pirate Pete isn't here.

Finally, you go to Tommo's Tattoo Table. You think that you're sure to find Pete there because it's the last place on your list of places pirates like to hang out. Tommo's table is in the square in the middle of Pirate Town, along with a number of other sellers. There's a stall that sells swashbuckling hats, a stall that sells butt-kicking boots, and an eel stew stall that makes your mouth water. You're glad you had those crumpets earlier.

Tommo specializes in temporary tattoos for pirates who don't like needles, and he's got some beauties on display: an anchor caught in the tentacles of a sea monster, a Jolly Roger skull and crossbones, and a heart with the word mom in it. You think about buying a dolphin tattoo for your friend Marina, but she spends so much time swimming that you worry it would wash off, and this is no time to be distracted.

Lots of pirates are lined up at Tommo's table, including one with gray striped pants, a patch on the right eye, and even a bit of a brown beard. However, she's also got a peg leg, and she's a lady. Pete is nowhere to be seen.

Now you're out of ideas. You've gone to all the places you know pirates like to go, and since those places were far apart, you've wasted a lot of time. What can you do now, but look everywhere else? That's going to take a long time, but the sooner you start, the sooner you'll finish, so you get to work. You go all over Pirate

Town, looking everywhere, marking off the places you've checked as you go. It takes several days, but finally you see him in the last place you expect.

You bump into Pete coming out of Made with Love Yarn Shop. You can see a crochet baby blanket sticking out of the top of his bag. He's just been to a meeting of his crochet club, which just goes to show that all pirates are different. You can't assume you know what someone likes to do in their spare time just because you know what their job is.

Pirate Pete gives you the treasure map and you take it back to Grandpa Pirate's house at last. "My boy!" he exclaims when you step into his parlor. "I thought you'd given up, but I see you have the treasure map. Good work."

"Thank you, sir," you say. "Finding Pirate Pete was difficult, but I found him in the end."

"You did, my boy, you did! However..." Grandpa Pirate hesitates.

"However?" you ask.

He goes on. "However, the pirate ship I was going to lend you to find the treasure, the Barnacle Bucket, has already left the harbor. She's set sail for Havana and won't be back for several months."

"Months!" you say.

"Months," he answers. "You'll just have to wait for it to return and then you can go in search of the treasure. There are lots of sneaky pirates in Pirate Town. Mind, you keep that map safe in the meantime."

"Aye aye," you reply.

Your decisions here had mixed results. You were cheated out of the map Grandpa Pirate gave you and you chased after the pirate who took it. This wasted a lot of time and was a pretty dangerous thing to do. You found Pirate Pete eventually, although you will have to wait to continue your quest.

This book has four different endings so if you haven't seen them all, you can:

Go back one step and choose not to redraw the map (turn to page 36).
Go back two steps and keep the map Grandpa Pirate gave you (turn to page 17).
Go back to the beginning and re-read the first scene (turn to page 1).
Or if you've read all four endings, turn to page 59.

You're back at the Pirate Prosthetics Shop. You have paper that the shopkeeper has given you in exchange for the tin you got from Percival the Pirate. This time you're going to make a different choice and you won't redraw the map.

DON'T REDRAW THE MAP

You decide not to draw a new map. You know Pirate Town well enough that you're sure you could draw the map if you wanted to, but what's the point? You already wasted a ton of time chasing Percival the Pirate all the way to the other side of Pirate Town. It's time to get to work looking for Pirate Pete.

You start out at places you know pirates

like, like the Sea Shanty Singalong and the Pirate Pet Pavilion. No luck, so then you expand your search and you check just about every street and alley, every shop and tavern in Pirate Town.

It's an exhausting hunt, and the worst part is that you accidentally check many places more than once. One tavern looks much like another. Each Pirate hat shop looks much like the next.

After days of looking, you go back to Grandpa Pirate's house in defeat. "I'm sorry, Grandpa Pirate," you say. "I've looked everywhere. I just can't find him." Actually, you're sure you missed some places in your hunt, but you don't know which places. You're discouraged and out of ideas.

Grandpa Pirate pats you on the shoulder. "That's a shame, my boy," he says. "The first thing a pirate needs to learn is to keep trying.

If something doesn't work, try again or try something different. Don't just give up."

"Yes, sir," you say, your head hanging.

"So you couldn't find Pirate Pete this time," says Grandpa Pirate. "It sounds like you're not ready to be a pirate captain yet."

You nod sadly.

He goes on. "But it's not the end of the world. You can try again next year."

"Thank you, Grandpa Pirate," you say and head home.

Your decisions here didn't work out so well. You were cheated out of the map Grandpa Pirate gave you and you chased after the pirate who took it. This wasted a lot of time and was a pretty dangerous thing to do. You decided not to redraw the map, which you thought would save time, but you forgot where you'd already been and visited some places more than once.

This book has four different endings so if you haven't seen them all, you can:

Go back one step and choose to redraw the map (turn to page 25).
Go back two steps and keep the map Grandpa Pirate gave you (turn to page 17).
Go back to the beginning and re-read the first scene (turn to page 1).
Or if you've read all four endings, turn to page 59.

You're back at Marina's cove. She's suggested you do a survey to find Pirate Pete. This time you're going to ask people specifically if they've seen him.

SURVEY - SPECIFIC

You decide to ask people specifically if they've seen Pirate Pete. This is a little risky, because you might tip off sneaky pirates that you're looking for him, but it will be faster than asking vague questions.

You ask fifty people if they've seen Pirate Pete recently, and if so, to mark where they saw him on the map. If they say they don't know

Pirate Pete, you tell them he is Grandpa Pirate's first mate. Some of them then say, "Oh yeah, I do know him," and mark where they've seen him. If they really don't know him, you then describe him: He has an eye patch on his right eye, a brown beard, and gray striped pants.

Of the fifty people you ask, only eleven say they've seen him recently. Apparently, he's been all over Pirate Town in the last few days, because the dots are scattered all over the map, but there are several at a business called Made With Love Yarn Shop so you decide to check there, even though it seems an unlikely place to find a pirate.

As you approach the store, you hear metal clanging, and getting closer, you see Pirate Pete and the sneaky pirate you met earlier fighting with cutlasses!

A cutlass is a short broad sword, slightly

curved, sharpened on one side and with a sharp point. You have your father's old cutlass at home, but you've never used it for sword fighting.

"Clang clang clang." The sneaky pirate keeps making cutting swings and Pirate Pete keeps blocking them.

"Get the bag, Pamela!" The sneaky pirate shouts, and his parrot dives and grabs a crochet bag sitting near Pirate Pete's feet. She flies off with it. The sneaky pirate flings sand toward Pirate Pete's eyes, turns, and runs away.

Pirate Pete starts after him, but he's going slow, rubbing at his one good eye. That's no problem, because a bunch of other pirates pour from the front of the shop and take off after the sneaky pirate, and they're quick.

They chase the sneaky pirate into a back alley. One of them throws a net crocheted from bright purple yarn, and it tangles around his feet, tripping him up. Another pirate wraps his arms around the sneaky pirate in a big bear hug, pinning his arms to his sides. You run up, take the cutlass from the sneaky pirate's sheath and hold it up in front of him. "Tell Pamela to bring back the bag!" you shout.

The pirate hesitates.

"You better do it, Percival," says Pirate Pete, walking up.

"Pamela, drop the bag," Percival, the sneaky pirate, calls to the bird circling overhead.

She does, and Pirate Pete catches it.

The pirates release Percival. He eyes the cutlass in your hand, but he knows pirate rules say it's yours now and he can't have it back. The parrot lands on his shoulder, and he walks away, head hanging.

"Yay!" The pirates around you shout.

"Nice job, kid," says one and pats you on the back.

"Thanks for the help, everyone," says Pirate Pete. "You can all go back in to Pirate Crochet Circle. I'll be there in a minute."

The other pirates leave you and Pirate Pete alone in the alley.

Pirate Pete pulls a half-finished rainbow-colored crochet baby blanket from his bag and looks it over. "Undamaged," he says. "Thanks for helping me get that back. I've put a lot of work into it."

You gape at him. "I thought the treasure map would be in there."

He laughs. "I wouldn't carry around a treasure map in my crochet bag." He pulls up his pant leg, takes the map out of the top of his boot, and hands it to you. "Be careful with that," he says.

You nod gravely, hide it in your own boot, and head to Grandpa Pirate's house.

Grandpa Pirate is very impressed to see you so soon. "That was the quickest I've ever seen, and you came back with a captured cutlass! You're a natural born pirate!" he exclaims.

"Thank you," you say smiling, but you know you can't take all the credit. "My friend Marina gave me the idea to do a survey, and the pirates from Pete's crochet circle helped catch the sneaky pirate, Percival, who was trying to steal the map."

Grandpa Pirate nods and smiles. "Everyone needs a little help sometimes, and a good pirate needs good friends. You're lucky to have Marina. You should invite her to go with you to find the treasure."

"Yes, definitely!" you say.

"How do you like that cutlass?" Grandpa

Pirate asks.

You look down at it and shrug. "It's heavy. It'll be a fine tool for cutting ropes and vines in the garden, but I'll leave it at home when I set sail. My father's old cutlass will serve me better at sea."

"A wise choice," says Grandpa Pirate with a nod. "Get yourself to the docks, boy! You'll find a ship called the Barnacle Bucket there. It'll need a little work, but then you can set sail to find the treasure."

"Hurrah!" you yell and jump into the air. "Thank you, Grandpa Pirate!" You head for the docks.

Your decisions have served you well. You used the map Grandpa Pirate gave you to help you conduct a survey where you asked people specifically if they'd seen Pete. This was a little risky and could have gone badly, but this time it worked out well. You found Pirate Pete in record time and captured a cutlass.

This book has four different endings so if you haven't seen them all, you can:

Go back one step and choose to ask people if they've seen someone who looks vaguely like Pirate Pete (turn to page 50).

Go back two steps and sell the map Grandpa Pirate gave you (turn to page 8).

Go back to the beginning and re-read the first scene (turn to page 1).

Or if you've read all four endings,

turn to page 59.

You're back at the cove with Marina. She's suggested you do a survey to find Pirate Pete. This time you're going to ask people if they've seen someone who looks vaguely like him.

SURVEY - VAGUE

You decide to ask people if they've seen someone vaguely fitting the description of Pirate Pete: a pirate with an eye patch, a beard, and striped pants. This may not be the fastest way to find him because Pete is not the only pirate matching that description, but it should be safe. No one will know exactly who you're looking for, so they won't be able to get to Pete before you do.

You ask 50 people if they've seen someone with an eye patch, a beard, and striped pants recently, and if so, to mark where they saw him on the map. Of the 50 people you ask, 23 say they've seen someone fitting that description. Apparently, Pete or his look-alikes have been all over Pirate Town in the last few days, because the dots are scattered all over the map, but there are a couple clusters of dots, one at Fantastic Figureheads and one at Made With Love Yarn Shop.

You decide to check Fantastic Figureheads first because every pirate ship needs a figurehead, so a workshop that makes and fixes them might be a good place to find a pirate.

There is only one person in the Fantastic Figureheads workshop when you get there.

A man is standing at the center of the room, using a chisel to carve a fantastic mermaid into wood. You see right away that this person fits your vague description, but he isn't Pirate Pete. He has an eye patch on his left eye, a red beard, red striped pants, and a name tag on his shirt that says "Sam."

Even though it's not Pete, you're so impressed by his carving that you stay a few minutes to watch. Lining the walls are color sketches of previous figureheads he's made—lions, unicorns, fancy women in flowing gowns, ancient heroes, dragons, sea serpents. Sam is a wonderful artist. As he works on his current carving, chip chip chipping with the chisel, bits of wood fall away, revealing the figure of the mermaid beneath. It's as if she was always there, hidden inside the wood.

"That's amazing," you tell him.

"Thanks, mate," he answers.

"When I'm captain of the Pickled Pearl, I'll have one of your figureheads on my bow," you vow before leaving the workshop and heading to Made With Love Yarn Shop.

The bells on the door jingle as you walk into the shop. The store smells wonderful, and you see that that's because there's a side table of refreshments with hot apple cider and ginger snaps. A sign says "Help Yourself," so you do. Delicious.

You wander through displays of many-colored yarn, knitting needles, crochet hooks, and homemade items such as dolls, stuffies, sweaters, and handbags. You hear people chatting.

At the back of the shop, you see a large round table, and seated around it are pirates—male pirates and female pirates, old pirates and young pirates, scowling pirates and smiling pirates—all crocheting. There's a pirate cat lounging in the center of the table, batting at a ball of yarn, and making a big tangle. You're so surprised, you accidentally knock over a display of pure alpaca wool. "Sorry," you say, "so sorry," and you start to pick it up.

"No problem, young man," says the shopkeeper. You know he runs the shop because of the Made With Love apron he's wearing. "Are you here for the pirate crochet circle?"

"No," you answer, "I'm here to speak with Pirate Pete."

At that, a man with an eye patch on his right eye, a brown beard, and gray striped pants stands, puts the rainbow-colored baby blanket he was working on into his bag, and comes toward you. "Found me already, did you? You made good time." Pirate Pete leads you toward the front of the shop where you and he can be alone. He pulls the map from his boot and gives it to you. You hide it in your own boot and head for Grandpa Pirate's house.

Grandpa Pirate smiles when you walk into his parlor. "Nice work getting the map," he says. "That was pretty fast."

"I can't take all the credit," you tell him. "Doing a survey and asking people where they'd seen someone fitting Pete's description was my friend Marina's idea."

"Marina is one smart mermaid. You should ask her to come with you on your quest to find the treasure."

"I will!" you say.

"It's too late today, but tomorrow morning you should go to the docks where you'll find the Barnacle Bucket, the ship I'm lending you for your quest to find the treasure. She'll need some work before she's ready to travel."

"Aye aye, Captain!" you say.

Your decisions worked out. You used the map Grandpa Pirate gave you to help you conduct a survey where you asked if people had seen someone vaguely like Pirate Pete. This was a safe choice, though it took you a little longer. You found Pirate Pete in good time.

This book has four different endings so if you haven't seen them all, you can:

Go back one step and choose to ask people specifically if they've seen Pirate Pete (turn to page 41).

Go back two steps and sell the map Grandpa Pirate gave you (turn to page 8).

Go back to the beginning and re-read the first scene (turn to page 1).

Or if you've read all four endings, turn to page 59.

A LITTLE BOOK OF **BIG** CHOICES

MATH PIRATES

MAKING A SAIL FOR A PIRATE SHIP

BOOK 2: ESTIMATION, AREA & BEGINNING GEOMETRY

S.E. BURR

MAKE YOUR OWN SAIL

Want to make your own sail for a pirate ship? Go to littlebooksofbigchoices. com and click the "Printables" link at the top of the page. On the Printables page, look for the worksheet on Making a Pirate Sail. You can download it, print it, and make your own sail!

MAKING A SAIL FOR A PIRATE SHIP

When you arrive at the dock, you see many large and impressive ships. It takes you a while to find the Barnacle Bucket, and when you do, you're a little disappointed. It clearly needs some help to be seaworthy. A couple pirates are hard at work with wood and tar patching holes in the sides. Also, the ship is missing one of its sails.

One of the pirates, a bald man with big muscles, sees you watching and waves. It's Uncle Six. He's called Six because he's exactly six feet tall. You wave back and with a speed and grace surprising for his size, he swings out on a long rope, lets go, does a somersault in the air, and then lands beside you on the dock. "You made it!"

You smile. "I made it."

"Great!" he says. "The next thing you need to do in Grandpa Pirate's quest is to get this old ship ready to sail."

"All right," you say. "Should I get some tar and help patch holes?"

"Not this time," he answers. "What we need you to do is get us a sail."

"A sail?" you say.

"A sail," he answers.

You think for a minute. You want to

seem smart and like you know what to do, but you really have no idea. "How?" you ask.

He hands you a small bag of coins. You weigh it in your hand, estimating how much gold it holds, but you're not great at estimating, so you loosen the strings and look inside. "This doesn't seem like very much gold to buy a whole sail with," you say.

He nods sympathetically. "And the more of that you spend, the less money you'll have for provisions for our voyage."

Your eyes widen. "This is for a sail and for provisions?"

He pats you on the shoulder. "A pirate quest is never easy, son."

"Okay…" you say.

He leans closer. "I'll give you a word of advice," he whispers.

"Please do," you whisper back.

"Buying a new sail will cost a lot," he says. "You'll save a lot of money if you sew it yourself."

You almost groan, but stop yourself. You hate sewing. "Okay," you say again. "Thanks, Uncle Six."

"You're welcome," he says and turns toward the gangplank.

"Wait!" you call after him. "What size sail do I need?"

"Sorry, son," Uncle Six answers. "You'll just have to figure that out for yourself." Then he springs up the gangplank and back onto the ship.

You stand on the dock for a minute thinking about what you should do. How will you know what size sail you need? Do you run home and get your aunt's measuring tape? If you did that, you'd have to climb up the mast to measure. You can do that, but it might take a lot of time, and you want to buy the fabric for the sail before the shops close.

You don't need to know the exact size. Like on all ships, this one has a range of sail sizes between the maximum (biggest) and minimum (smallest) sails that would work. You can estimate the size. As you stand there, you realize that Uncle Six is standing right next to the mast with the missing sail. Uncle Six is a hard worker. He doesn't usually just stand around, so what's he doing?

And then it occurs to you! You pull the pencil Grandpa Pirate gave you from your pocket and hold it up in front of your face. Since Uncle Six is far away and the pencil is up close, he looks like he's the same height as the pencil. You measure the mast from this perspective and see that it looks like it's three pencil lengths. That means that it's about 18 feet high because Uncle Six is six feet tall and three times six is 18.

Seeing that you've figured out what he's up to, Uncle Six yawns dramatically and lays down beneath the missing sail's boom. You smile and measure the boom using your pencil and find that it's a little over one and a half Uncle Sixes, meaning it's about 10 feet. So now you know that the sail's luff (height) is about 18 feet and the sail's foot (bottom edge) is about 10 feet. You've got the measurements you need. You turn and walk back up the dock toward Pirate Town.

You need to decide where to buy the fabric, and the way you see it, you have two choices.

The cheapest place for you to find the fabric you need is likely to be the Flotsam

Flea Market. The problem is that you never know what you'll find at the flea market, and you might not find the best sailcloth there. You may have to piece your sail together from used clothes. That sort of patchwork sail would require a lot of time sewing, and likely wouldn't be as good as a sail made from bigger sheets of sailcloth. On the other hand, you may find just what you're looking for and save a lot of money.

Your other option is to buy the fabric at Fortune Fabrics. The fabric for sale at that shop is expensive. However, you're almost certain to find sailcloth there that will be easy to sew and will make a strong, lightweight sail.

So what do you do?

Do you go to Flotsam Flea Market (turn to page 72)?

or

Do you go to Fortune Fabrics (turn to page 83)?

You're back on the dock, and Uncle Six has given you money to buy fabric for a sail. This time you're going to make a different choice and head to Flotsam Flea Market.

THE FLOTSAM FLEA MARKET

The Flotsam Flea market is an open-air market made up of a bunch of cobbled together stalls of all sizes and shapes. You can buy pirate plunder of all sorts, and if you take the time to hunt through it all, you can get some great bargains.

As you walk into the market an array of smells hits your nose: frying fish, herbs and spices, the dung of horses and sheep, hay, and a thousand other smells that you can't identify but that fill you with excitement. The Flotsam Market is always fun.

As you wander between the stalls, you see many wonderful things, and you wish you could spend the money in your pouch how you like instead of saving it for a sail and provisions. But maybe this itself is a test. A true captain puts the needs of the ship first. But there are so many temptations!

One booth sells nothing but toys. There are ball and cup games, tops painted in bright colors, and stick ponies. The ponies' heads are carved and painted so realistically that you expect them to neigh and nip at you as you walk by.

A clothes seller has many, many striped shirts. You love striped shirts. They're so fashionable! You would look like such a dashing pirate captain if you had one! Oh well. You stop at the clothes seller, though, to see if he has anything that could be sewn together to make a sail. Imagine a sail made of a patchwork of striped shirts! But you know that that would take too long to sew, and the shirts cost too much to be used that way, anyway.

Movement above catches your eye and you glimpse the bright feathers of a flying parrot. You make eye contact with the bird. It's looking right at you! Lots of Pirates have parrots. They're not rare in Pirate Town, but this one looks an awful lot like Pamela the Parrot, the pet of Percival the sneaky Pirate. Percival and Pamela are a very tricky duo, and you know they would do anything to get your treasure map and the treasure it leads to.

You don't see Percival, but if Pamela's

here, he probably is too. He's probably hiding nearby and watching you. You need to lose them, so you cut through a stall selling fish pies and out the back. Then you hurry, weaving this way and that between stalls. You cut through another stall, this one selling designer eye patches. "Hey what do you think you're doing?" the seller calls out as you hurry by.

"Sorry," you say and keep going.

You think you must have lost Percival and the parrot, so you stop to catch your breath, and you see something really interesting at the front of a stall. A ship inside a bottle! It's a small model ship, sure, but it's still way too big to have fit through the opening in the bottle. "How on earth did they get it in there?" you ask.

The seller laughs. "That's a mystery," he says, and then turns back to another customer.

"Maybe they built it inside there,"

whispers a girl standing next to you. She has long brown hair in two braids, and she's wearing a great striped shirt.

"No way," you answer. "They couldn't get their hands inside the bottle to build it."

"Maybe they have special, long, thin tools they used to build it inside there," she says.

"Oh!" you say, "maybe so."

"Or," she goes on, "maybe they have little hinges at the bottom of the masts and they put the ship into the bottle with the masts all folded down so it'll fit through the bottleneck. Then, when they get it in there, they use a string to pull the masts up."

"Oh my! You may be right. You're really smart," you tell her. She may even be as smart as your friend Marina.

"Thanks," she says. "I'm Becky."

"I'm Patrick," you answer.

Just then, the parrot you saw earlier swoops down and lands on Becky's shoulder.

"Oh, no!" you say.

"What?" she asks.

"Is that Pamela?" you ask. "Do you know Percival the Pirate?"

"Who?" she asks and then she says, "No, this is just my parrot, Polly."

"Polly?" you ask.

"Polly," she answers.

"That's a relief," you say and wipe your forehead. You were starting to sweat.

"What are you looking for at the market?" she asks.

"Cloth for a sail," you answer, "but I'm not having much luck."

She smiles. "Your luck has just turned."

"What?" you ask.

"Follow me," she says. "I know just the

thing."

You follow her to a stand at the edge of the market. It sells dishes, silverware, and best of all, used tablecloths. "What size do you need?" she asks.

"The mast is 18 feet, and the boom is ten feet," you say.

"We should take off two feet in both directions to make sure it's not too big," she says.

"Right," you agree.

She rummages through a crate sitting on the ground, and pulls out a stack of matching white tablecloths, which are heavily stained with food. They have a note pinned to them telling their size and price. They're square, eight feet by eight feet, and the price is very reasonable.

"Can we lay these out on the beach to see how they'll fit?" Becky asks the seller and gestures to the beach beyond his stall.

He shrugs. "Sure. Not like they can get much dirtier."

Becky and you lay out two tablecloths on the beach. "There," she says. "That's your rectangular sail: 16 by eight."

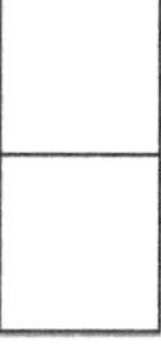

"It's a triangular sail," you tell her.

She smiles and pulls a long string from her pocket. "Hold that at the corner," she says.

You do, and she hands you one end of the string and then goes to the corner diagonally across from you and pulls the string tight so it makes a line, cutting the rectangle into two triangles. Or two triangular sails! "An eight by eight tablecloth is 64 square feet. Once you cut it and piece it together, you'll only need one of these tablecloths to make your sail."

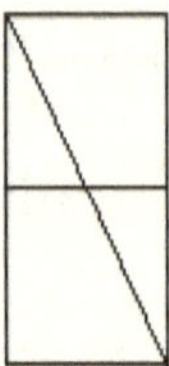

"That's great!" you say.

"Who's going to sew it?" she asks.

You shrug. "I will. I can sew and I'll ask my aunt to help." You CAN sew, but you're not very good at it, and your aunt isn't either, but you're sure she'll help if you ask her.

"You could do that..." she says, "or..."

"Or what?" you ask.

"I'll help you," she says. "I'm a great sewer. I have the second fastest needle in Pirate

Town. I'll have your sail done in no time, and all it'll cost you is a second tablecloth."

"You want a tablecloth?" you ask.

She nods. "I need a new sail, too. What do you say?"

You stop and think. Should you buy a second tablecloth for Becky so she'll help you sew the sail? This will undoubtedly save time. It'll cost you more, but the tablecloths are pretty cheap. You think you can afford it with enough money left over for provisions.

Or will you ask your aunt to help you? This is free, but will take longer and you might mess it up. Neither of you are very good at sewing.

Ask Becky for help (turn to page 94).

or

Ask your aunt for help (turn to page 104).

You're back on the dock, and Uncle Six has given you money to buy fabric for a sail. This time you're going to make a different choice and head to Fortune Fabrics.

FORTUNE FABRICS

You walk into Fortune Fabrics, Pirate Town's only fabric shop, and you can't help but be excited by all the stripes you see—brown stripes, red stripes, blue stripes, black stripes, gold stripes. You're a pirate who likes to be fashionable, and what's more fashionable than stripes? Striped shirts, striped pants, striped hats—you love them all. You would even wear striped shoes if they made them. They don't, but maybe they should. What an exciting idea! You could paint stripes onto the leather!

You close your eyes, blocking out all the beautiful stripes, and take a deep breath. This is no time to get distracted. You're here for a sail and unfortunately sailcloth isn't striped.

But why is that?

Wouldn't that look great?

A fashionable sail for a fashionable pirate?

You shake your head and take another deep breath. You need to make a sail quickly and cheaply. That means no stripes.

Opening your eyes, you see the shop keeper looking at you. She is wearing lots of stripes, and lots of gold and pearls, too. She looks fashionable and rich, which doesn't bode well for you getting a good deal. Clearly she makes big profits selling fabric.

"Are you well, young man?" she asks.

"Yes, quite well," you answer, "just a bit overwhelmed with all the stripes."

She laughs. "Yes. Yes! I sell some wonderful stripes. My name is Madame Dubois. How can I help you?"

"I need fabric to make a sail," you say.

"Excellent!" she replies. "You've come to the right place." She pulls a bolt of white fabric from the shelf and partly unrolls it. "Feel this," she says.

You do.

Madame Dubois goes on. "This here is premium sailcloth, nothing stronger or lighter. You can sail a galleon with this. Nice, isn't it?"

You nod. "Very nice, but I don't need a sail for a galleon. I just need a sail for a small schooner."

"Just because your ship is small doesn't mean it's not special," says Madame Dubois. "Quality cloth means quality sailing. Make your sail from this and you'll be amazed by how fast and nimble your little boat can be."

Nimble isn't the first word that comes to mind when you think of the Barnacle Bucket, but maybe it could be. Perhaps she's right. On the other hand, the sack of coins your uncle gave you is very light. If you buy that you won't have money for provisions and you'll starve on your way to find the treasure. "I don't have much money," you tell her. "I need inexpensive cloth."

Just then the bell on the door jingles behind you, and the shopkeeper gives a wide smile. "Captain Martin!" she calls.

"Just have a look around," she says to you

as she walks away.

You look around, but do not know where to start.

"Psst, lad," someone says, and you think of that sneaky pirate, Percival and his parrot Pamela.

You see the person talking to you and it's not Percival or Pamela. It's another pirate, a friendly looking female pirate sitting at a table near the back of the shop. "Aye?" you say.

She beckons you closer.

You see several other pirates seated at the table with her, all sewing. This must be a pirate sewing circle. You aren't surprised. Grandpa Pirate's first mate, Pirate Pete, is in a pirate crochet circle. Pirates can have all different kinds of hobbies.

The pirate lady says, "The discount fabric is over there," and she points to a rack. "What you want is that one on the bottom left."

You look at the price pinned to the bolt, and she's right. It's much more affordable than the fabric that Madame Dubois showed you. However, it's not a full bolt. "Will there be enough?" you ask.

"How much do you need?" the pirate asks.

You blush. "I'm not sure," you say.

"Do you have the measurements of the mast and the boom?" she asks.

You nod. "The mast is about 18 feet and the boom is 10."

"All right," she says and pulls out a scrap of paper. "Anyone got a pencil?"

You take your pencil from your pocket and hand it to her.

"You don't want your sail to be too big," she says, "and it doesn't have to keep the same proportions." She taps her chin with the pencil. "We'll take two feet off each side. That way it won't be too big and it won't be too small either."

She draws a rectangle on the paper and marks the tall side 16 and the bottom side 8.

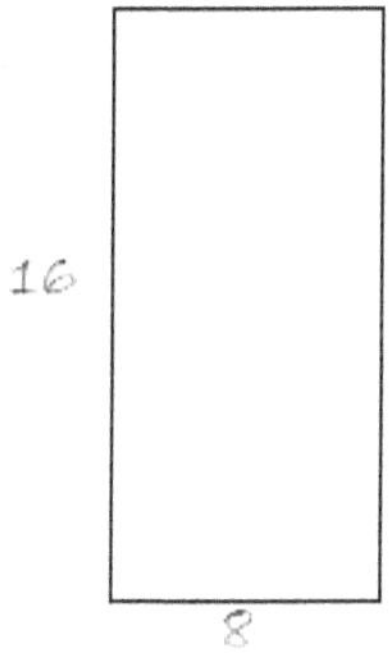

"To know how many square feet of fabric you need, you can draw squares—16 by 8." She draws lines in the rectangle to make a bunch of squares. "If you count the squares you'll know how many square feet you need," she says.

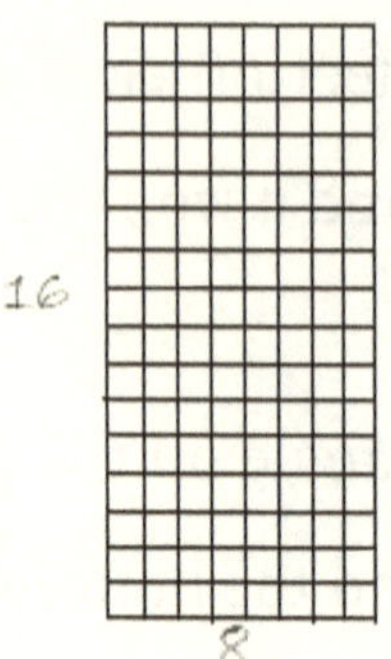

You start to count.

She interrupts you, "Or you can just multiply the height by the width. 16 times eight equals 128 square feet of fabric for a rectangular sail with those dimensions." She eyes the fabric bolt. "You may not have enough."

"It's a triangular sail," you tell her.

"Oh good," she says, and draws a diagonal line from the top left to the bottom right of the rectangle. Now her drawing looks like two identical sails, one right side up and one upside down. "A triangular sail with those measurements will take half as much fabric as a rectangular one. One hundred twenty-eight square feet divided by two means you'll need 64 square feet for your sail." She looks again at the bolt of fabric. "That's plenty," she says. "I think you've found your sailcloth."

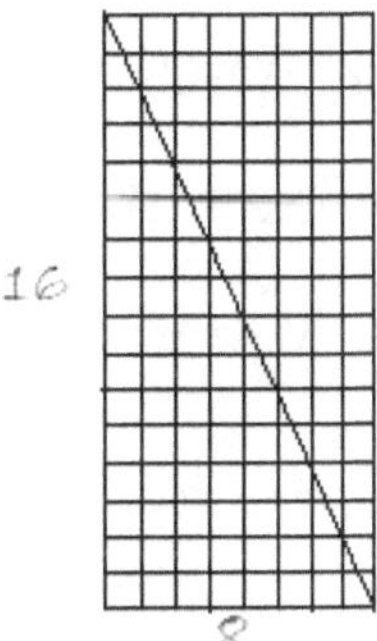

You smile. "Thank you so much!"

She smiles back. "Do you need help sewing your sail? Our circle was just saying that it's been a while since we had a big project to work on together. We'd be happy to help you with it."

"I'm happy to help, too," says Madame Dubois, walking up. Her other customer has left. "In addition to selling fabric I offer my services as a seamstress, and I've got the fastest needle in Pirate Town. Hire me and you'll have your sail ready in half the time it'll take if you work with these amateurs."

"That's true," said the pirate, "if you can pay for it. What do you want to do?"

Do you ask the sewing circle to help you make the sail (turn to page 114)?

or

Do you hire Madame Dubois (turn to page 121)?

You're back on the beach with Becky, and this time you're going to make a different choice and ask her to help you make the sail.

ASK BECKY FOR HELP

You decide to ask Becky to help you sew the sail.

It'll cost you a little more to buy the second tablecloth, but you saved so much money by shopping at the Flotsam Flea Market that you can afford it. Your only other idea is to ask your aunt to help you, and she's not very good at sewing. It would take the two of you a long time and you might mess it up. This way you think it'll be done fast and it'll be done right.

"Where should we go to sew it?" you ask.

She shrugs. "Why not right here?"

"Here?" You ask, surprised. "Outside on the beach?"

"Exactly," she answers. "The tide doesn't reach here. We won't get the fabric wet, or get it washed out to sea or anything."

"I know," you say, feeling embarrassed. You're not sure why you're so surprised by the idea of outdoor sewing. "It's just that I've only ever seen people sew indoors."

"Anything you can do inside is more fun outside," she says.

"Anything?" you ask.

She laughs. "Maybe not anything, but most things, and definitely sewing."

"The sail might blow away," you say.

She licks her finger and holds it up, testing the wind. "Maybe in a storm, but not in this gentle breeze."

"Hmm." You think about it for a moment. "All right. Let's do it here."

"Great," she answers. "Now go pay the seller."

You do, and then Becky and you get to work making your sail.

She folds the tablecloth in half and uses your pencil to mark the center of the top edge where the fold is. Then she lays it back out flat and draws a straight line between the mark and the corner of the tablecloth.

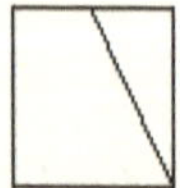

She pulls a pair of scissors from her pocket. Polly, who has been hopping around and digging at the sand with her beak, says "Pretty!" and makes a move toward the scissors.

"Don't even think about it," says Becky. The bird gives her a long, offended stare and then goes back to digging in the sand.

Becky cuts along the line she drew. "Polly likes shiny things."

"Gold!" Polly squawks.

Becky starts sewing the piece she cut onto the top edge of the other piece.

"What do I do?" you ask.

"Do the same thing I just did to the other

tablecloth," she answers. "That one's yours."

"That one's mine?" you ask. "I thought this one was mine."

She shakes her head. "I'm making my sail first."

"Oh," is all you say.

"Don't worry," she tells you. "I'll have both sails done in less time than it would have taken you to make one."

She's probably right. You carefully copy the steps she took on the first tablecloth. You ask her to check your line before you cut it.

She tells you it's fine. The line you cut isn't completely straight, but you take your time and do your best.

Finishing the seam on her sail, she looks at yours. "Good enough," she says and starts to sew it.

Both sails are quickly finished. Becky

stands. "Come on, Polly!" she says.

The bird ignores her.

She whistles. Nothing. "Polly!" Still nothing.

You grow suspicious. "Pamela!" you say, and the bird squawks and looks your way.

Becky chuckles. "You caught me," she says, and then, "Pamela, come!"

The bird flies up and perches on her shoulder.

"I knew I recognized her!" you say.

"Yep," she says. "Percival the Pirate is my papa."

"That sneaky pirate is your papa!" you say.

"Yep," she says, "I'm his daughter."

You look at the new sail she's holding.

"Are you going to take my sail from me after I helped you make yours?" she asks.

"No," you say, frowning. "You earned it fair and square."

"Good," she says. "Thanks for the fabric. We needed to get our boat in good working order to go after that treasure."

"What treasure?" you ask.

She winks. "That one you've got a map for."

"What!" you say, shocked. "How do you know where it is?"

"I don't," she answers, "but you do."

"And you're planning to follow me," you say, "and I helped you get the sail you need to do it."

She shrugs. "Don't feel bad," she says. "If you hadn't bought me the fabric, I would have gotten a new sail one way or another."

She turns and starts walking away. She looks back. "I'll see you soon," she says.

A chill runs down your back. You got your sail quickly and cheaply, but you're in trouble. Becky, Percival's daughter, is sneaky just like he is.

Your decisions here worked out well. You got the fabric you needed cheaply, and you have a good working sail, though it's dirty. Becky tricked you, but there was no harm done. You're sure that she would have gotten the sail she needed, with or without you. You have plenty of money left for provisions, but you'll look for good deals, anyway. Pirates should be thrifty, after all.

You successfully completed this step in your quest. You're worried about what Percival and Becky are up to, so you'll keep a careful eye out for them as you continue your quest and set sail to find the treasure.

This book has four different endings so if you haven't seen them all, you can:

Go back one step and ask your aunt to help you make the sail (turn to page 103).
Go back two steps and go to Fortune Fabrics rather than Flotsam Flea Market
(turn to page 82).
Go back to the beginning and re-read the first scene (turn to page 63).
Or if you've read all four endings,
turn to page 125.

You're back on the beach with Becky, and this time you're going to make a different choice and ask your aunt for help making the sail.

ASK YOUR AUNT FOR HELP

"Thank you for helping me find a good deal on fabric and for helping me figure out how much I need," you say to Becky. You pause. You feel a little guilty, because she's helped you a lot, but you need to save as much money as you can for provisions. Besides, you're a little suspicious. Her parrot, Polly, looks an awful lot like Pamela, Percival's parrot. You go on. "I'm going to ask my aunt to help me sew the sail. I need to save as much money as I can."

Becky grimaces. She looks mad, but then she shrugs and smiles. "All right," she says. "I'll get the sail I need another way."

You nod and turn away. "See you around," you call.

"See you!" says Becky.

"See you!" squawks the parrot.

You pay for the tablecloth and head to your aunt's house.

It's a nice little place that she maintains herself. She's good with her hands. The house has a great garden full of vegetables, fruits, and lots of flowers. That's where you find your aunt.

"You want me to help you sew your sail?" she asks, standing and brushing her dirty hands on her apron. "You know I'm bad at sewing, right?"

You nod. "I'm bad at it, too."

Aunt Penny laughs. "Then shouldn't you ask someone for help who knows what they're doing?"

"I need to save as much money as I can for provisions," you tell her.

She nods. Your aunt has powerful feelings about properly provisioned ships. "All right," she says. "Let's give it a try."

You lay the tablecloth flat on the floor of the kitchen.

"How do we turn this square cloth into a triangular sail?" Aunt Penny asks.

"Hmm." You remember how Becky used a string to mark a diagonal line from one corner of the rectangle she laid out to the other. You do the same with the square and draw a line from one corner to another. Then you cut it.

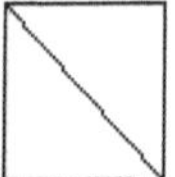

"Now what?" Aunt Penny asks. "How do the pieces go together?"

You try a few arrangements, but it's hopeless. They don't fit. You have two triangular sails, both half as big as you need. You've made a mistake.

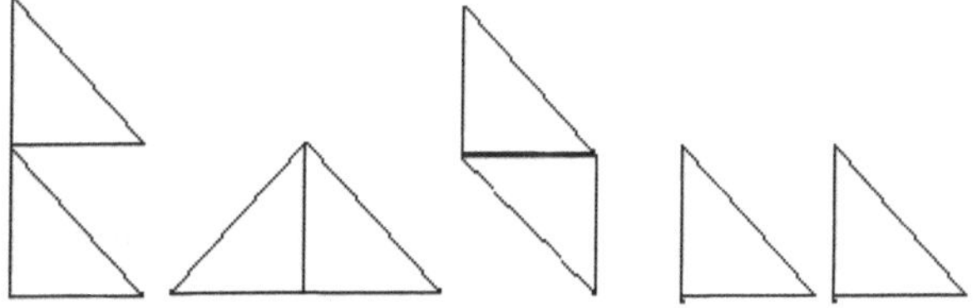

"Let's sit down with a piece of paper and figure this out," your aunt says. Drawing on the paper, you work out that the cut should have gone from the center of the top edge to the bottom corner.

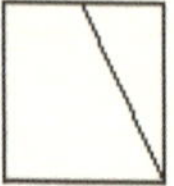

"Maybe we can sew the pieces back together and cut again?" you ask.

"We could..." she says. "But it'll take a long time since we're not very good sewers. Could you get another tablecloth?"

You nod. "Yes. They're not very expensive. I'll go get another."

You go back to the booth where you bought the first tablecloth and try to buy another one, but the seller gives you a price that is double what you paid before. You ask him why.

"That's the price for two," he says. "The one you're buying now and the one your friend took."

"My friend?" you ask.

"Becky," he answers. "She said you'd pay for it when you came back."

"What!" you exclaim. "I told her I wouldn't buy one for her!"

"That's not what she said," says the man. "Was she lying?"

"Yes!" you answer.

The man makes a tutting sound. "That girl is as sneaky as her father."

"Who's her father?" you ask.

"Percival the Pirate," he answers. "Didn't you recognize the parrot?"

You don't know what to say. You did recognize it, but she said its name was Polly. You feel very foolish for being tricked. That's one sneaky girl. You take a deep breath. "I didn't tell her I'd pay for hers. Can I just have this one at the regular price?"

He shakes his head. "Sorry. You want it, you'll have to pay for both."

Grumbling, you pull the money from your pouch and pay for two tablecloths. Now you've bought three when you should have only needed one. You got a good price for them so you should still have enough money for provisions but you'll have to be thrifty. It takes you and your aunt quite a bit of time to do the sewing, but you finish eventually.

Your decisions here had mixed results. You bought three tablecloths when you only needed one. This was both because of Becky's trickery, and because you didn't know what you were doing and messed up your first attempt at making a sail. You got a working sail in the end, though it's dirty, inexpertly sewn, and it took a long time to make. You'll have to look for good deals in order to provision your boat, but you would have done that anyway. Pirates should be thrifty, after all.

You successfully completed this step in your quest. You're worried about what Percival and Becky are up to, so you'll keep a careful eye out for them as you continue your quest and set sail to find the treasure.

This book has four different endings so if you haven't seen them all, you can:

Go back one step and ask Becky to help you
make the sail (turn to page 93).
Go back two steps and go to Fortune Fabrics
rather than Flotsam Flea Market
(turn to page 82).
Go back to the beginning and re-read the first
scene (turn to page 63).
Or if you've read all four endings,
turn to page 125.

You're back at Fortune Fabrics, and this time you're going to make a different choice and ask the pirate sewing circle to help you make the sail.

ASK THE PIRATE SEWING CIRCLE FOR HELP

You decide to ask the pirate sewing circle for help making the sail. The fabric you buy is four feet wide and 16 feet long.

Madame Dubois scowls at you as she rings up your fabric. It's a much better deal than the fabric she originally showed you, but it's still pretty expensive. If you had paid her for sewing too, you might not have had enough money for provisions.

With the pirates' help, you work out what you're going to do on a scrap of paper before marking and cutting the fabric. You will cut from the top right corner to the center of the left edge. This will make a triangle, which you will then sew onto the bottom half of the right edge.

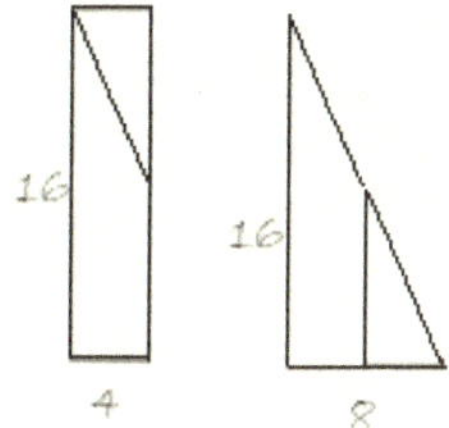

You get to work, and it goes fairly quickly. Somehow the fabric gets twisted and one of the pirates ends up sewing the wrong sides together so you have to pick out a bunch of stitches. You take a deep breath to control your frustration.

If there is any task in the world more irksome than stitch-picking, you don't know what it is.

But it all comes together in the end, and you have a really wonderful sail. You're sure it's nicer and cleaner than what you would have ended up with if you'd gotten your fabric from the flea market. You spent quite a bit on the fabric and now you spend a little more to buy the pirate sewing circle a spool of thread as a thank you. You'll have to be as thrifty as possible on the provisions, but everyone knows you should keep groups of pirates on your good side, and they helped you. You're grateful.

"Thanks, guys!" you say and head back toward the dock, your sail in your arms.

On your way to the Barnacle Bucket, you nearly bump into a girl carrying her own sail, hers a little dingy looking and stained. She clearly made it from second hand fabric.

A parrot squawks and takes off from her shoulder, and you stop and watch. You think you recognize it. Is that Pamela?

The parrot flies to a nearby boat and lands on a man's shoulder. It's Percival the Pirate! Percival doesn't seem to recognize you. "You got the sail, Becky?"

"Aye, aye, papa!" The girl calls.

She sees you looking at her and winks at you before heading up the gangplank and onto the boat.

You hurry away. *Oh, no!* you think. That sneaky pirate, Percival, and his daughter, Becky, are getting a boat ready to sail just like you are. You have a terrible suspicion that they're after the same treasure.

Your decisions here had mixed results. You spent more than you would have liked on the fabric. You'll have to look for the best deals possible in order to provision your boat, but you would have done that anyway. Pirates should be thrifty, after all. You got a good sail and successfully completed this step in your quest. You're worried about what Percival and Becky are up to, so you'll keep a careful eye out for them as you continue your quest and set sail to find the treasure.

This book has four different endings so if you haven't seen them all, you can:

Go back one step and choose to hire Madame Dubois to make the sail (turn to page 120).

Go back two steps and go to the Flotsam Flea Market rather than Fortune Fabrics (turn to page 71).

Go back to the beginning and re-read the first scene (turn to page 63).

Or if you've read all four endings, turn to page 125.

You're back at Fortune Fabrics, and this time you're going to make a different choice and hire Madame Dubois to make the sail for you.

ASK MADAME DUBOIS TO MAKE THE SAIL

You decide to hire Madame Dubois to make the sail. You're terrible at sewing, and you hate doing it. You're certain that she can get it done much faster than you can, even with the pirate sewing circle's help.

And you're right. She cuts the fabric quickly and then sews. She's so fast that you can barely see the needle! It's amazing! You and the other pirates watch in wonder. This is a sight to behold! She's done in no time. The sail looks great! But then she rings up the charge for the finished sail, and you groan. You try to haggle, offering her a lower price, but it's no good. Sadly, you open the money pouch and give it all to her.

Then, carrying the sail, you walk to Grandpa Pirate's house. You find him in the parlor. "My boy!" he says in surprise. "I didn't expect to see you today. What's wrong?"

You tell him you spent all the money Uncle Six gave you on the sail and you have nothing left for provisions.

Grandpa Pirate frowns. "That's too bad," he says. "You've failed this part of your quest. Your first task, finding Pirate Pete, tested your speed. This task tested how good you were at finding deals and saving money. A pirate has to be thrifty, you know?"

You nod and look at the floor.

"Give me that sail and your map," Grandpa Pirate says.

You do.

"I'll keep these safe for you," he says and squeezes your shoulder. "I think you're not quite ready to be a pirate captain yet, but you can try again next year."

"Thank you, Grandpa Pirate," you say. You have to wait a whole year, but at least you get a second chance.

Your decisions here didn't work out very well. You spent all the money you had. You have nothing left for provisions, so you can't set sail in search of the treasure. You have to wait a whole year to try again.

This book has four different endings so if you haven't seen them all, you can:

Go back one step and choose to ask the pirate sewing circle to help make the sail (turn to page 113).

Go back two steps and go to the Flotsam Flea Market rather than Fortune Fabrics (turn to page 71).

Go back to the beginning and re-read the first scene (turn to page 63).

Or if you've read all four endings, turn to page 125.

MATH PIRATES

PIRATE PROVISIONS

S.E. BURR

PIRATE PROVISIONS

You get up bright and early and head to Pirate Town Farm.

The owner of the farm is Grandpa Pirate's sister, which makes her either your grand-aunt or your great-aunt, depending on who you ask. She greets you with a hug. She smells of hay, sweat, and a bit of cow manure. "It's good to see you, Nephew," she says.

"It's good to see you too, Aunt Farmer," you answer.

"Come inside and have breakfast," she says. "I have some porridge still hot in the pot and I can fry you up some eggs in no time."

"Yes, please." Aunt Farmer is one of the best cooks you know, and she has some of the freshest, best tasting food in Pirate Town. You sit down and eat porridge with fresh goats' milk and a plate of eggs. At the end of the meal, your stomach is bursting. "Thank you, ma'am," you say. "That was delicious."

"My pleasure," she says, "and now I reckon you'll be wanting to have a look at the animals. I hear you're about to leave on an adventure."

"Yes, ma'am," you say.

You need to choose what kind of animals to take on your voyage. Food spoils fast on a pirate ship, so lots of ships keep farm animals to provide fresh food. Once you get your ship provisioned, you'll set sail in search of hidden treasure. But you're not only interested in the animals that might sail with you. You've always loved the farm.

"Hello, Bess," you say to the chestnut mare, the first animal to greet you. You let her smell your fingers and then rub her neck. The two of you are old friends.

Next the donkeys, Duke and Duchess, say hello. Duke lifts his top lip, showing you his teeth and smells you.

You throw bread crumbs over a short fence to the ducks. When you run out of crumbs, one duck tries to get to you through the fence to see if you have more. The spaces between the slats of the fence are too small for her to pass through, but she keeps trying. You feel sorry for the silly thing and step sideways to the gate that's been open all along. Aunt Farmer's ducks are none too smart. The duck nibbles at your empty hand with her bill and you stroke her soft, smooth feathers.

"I recommend either goats or chickens for your boat," says Aunt Farmer.

The goats are funny and very smart. As you watch, a small goat leaps onto a bigger one's back and peers at you over the fence. Another one jumps onto the swing that Aunt Farmer has put up for them, a four-foot-long board held by four ropes. That silly billy swings back and forth. He's having a great time.

"Lots of ships have goats," Aunt Farmer says. "They have excellent sea legs and keep their balance easily on a rocking ship. If they get knocked overboard, they're excellent swimmers. They're also nice pets and fun to have around. But on the downside, they eat a lot of food, and they take up a lot of space."

"How much space?" you ask.

"You'll want two goats, I think," she says. "You can't have just one or she'll get lonely. Each goat will need 20 square feet resting space and 30 square feet exercise space."

"All right," you say and do the math. "Two goats times twenty square feet each equals 40 square feet resting space in the hold."

"That's right," she says.

You go on. "Two goats times thirty square feet each equals 60 square feet exercise space. 60 square feet exercise space plus 40 square feet resting space equals 100 square feet." You shake your head. "I can't spare that much space in my hold. The Barnacle Bucket is a small schooner. I need space to store food and for the crew to sleep."

Aunt Farmer nods. "You don't need their exercise space to be in the hold. It can be up on deck. They'll have no trouble climbing the stairs to get up there. So, you'll need their 40 square feet resting space to be below deck, plus the space to hold their food. They'll each need three pounds of hay per day, a little less if you have lots of food scraps from the galley."

"What about chickens?" you ask.

She leads you to the chicken coop. They're outside, walking around, scratching at the ground and pecking at it, looking for bits of grain. The little yellow chicks are adorable, but you can't take any babies. You need hens who will start laying eggs immediately.

"Chickens take up less space," she tells you. "You only need 2 square feet per chicken inside the coop. Some sailors build the coop up on deck to save even more space in the hold, but the chickens can get a little wet that way, and I've heard of coops getting washed overboard in a severe storm."

"Can they swim?" you ask.

She shakes her head sadly. "You need to keep your birds safe."

You nod solemnly.

"I think you'll want five chickens. That's 10 square feet in the coop since five chickens times two square feet each equals 10 square feet."

"What about their exercise space?" you ask.

She nods. "They'll each need 10 square feet exercise space, so 10 square feet each times five chickens equals fifty square feet. However, just like the goats, the chickens' exercise space can be up on deck. I think they'll be able to climb the stairs, too, no problem."

You nod. "And if they can't, I can always carry them up the stairs for their outside time."

"Right," she says. "Chickens are a lot lighter than goats."

"How much do they eat?" you ask.

"They each will need a quarter pound of feed per day," she answers.

"So that's what?" you say, working it out. "Four quarters makes one pound, so for five chickens, that's one and a quarter pounds of feed per day."

"Correct," Aunt Farmer answers. "So, what do you think?" she asks. "Do you want hens or nanny goats?"

"I can't have both?" you ask.

"You don't have space for both," she answers.

You sigh. "All right. I know what I want."

Do you choose chickens (turn to page 146)?

or

Do you choose goats (turn to page 137)?

You're back on the farm with Aunt Farmer, and this time you're going to make a different choice. You choose two nanny goats.

YOU CHOOSE GOATS

You choose goats. The goats seem cuter than the chickens, and you'll enjoy having furry friends aboard the ship. Also, it'll be nice having fresh milk while at sea.

Aunt Farmer gives you a white goat named Daisy and a black goat named Midnight. They're both female, a.k.a. nanny goats, because you need them for their milk. Although goats have a reputation for being stubborn, these two are friendly and curious. As you put a lead rope on each of them and lead them from the pen, they seem excited to be going on an adventure.

You and the goats walk through town and to the dock. You lead them up the gangplank of the Barnacle Bucket.

"Daisy! Midnight!" calls Uncle Six, seeing the goats. He comes over to say hello. "I'm glad you ladies will sail with us." He feeds them each a bit of carrot. "I've often told Aunt Farmer that you are the nicest pair of nannies I've ever had the privilege of knowing."

The goats seem pleased with Uncle Six's flattery. They each have their ears forward and their tails up, meaning they're in a good mood. It always pays to be polite to goats.

"I'm working on getting the water barrels filled," Uncle Six says. "I'll start bringing them down into the hold soon."

"Great!" you say. "Thank you. The ladies and I will be down in the hold setting up their living arrangements."

"Did Aunt Farmer tell you how much space they'll need?" he asks.

"She said twenty square feet per goat for resting, so forty square feet for the two of them."

"Hmm," he says. "Forty square feet, aye?"

"Aye," you answer.

"I reckon we need nine barrels of water," Uncle Six says. "We can refill the water when we get to the island. We'll need eighteen barrels of food, nine for the way there and nine for the way back. This is a small schooner. It might be a tight fit."

"Right" you answer, frowning. "Well, if you put the water barrels in the hold, we'll have a better idea of how the food barrels will fit."

"Aye Aye, captain!" Uncle Six says.

You smile as he walks away. "Captain." That sounds awfully nice.

You lead the goats to the staircase, which goes down to the hold. You're worried, but they make it down the stairs, no problem, and you're sure they'd be able to climb back up just as easily.

The hold is currently empty except for the bunks, so you let them wander freely while you construct their living quarters. All they really need is an area to keep them contained and out of trouble at night, so you decide to make them a small pen at one end of the hold. You measure it out. It's eight feet in one direction and five in the other. This comes out to 40 square feet since eight times five is 40. You build a fence with a gate.

As you work, Uncle Six brings down the

water barrels one by one. This takes up more and more of the space in the hold, so you bring the goats into their pen to get them out of the way.

You go to the market to buy fresh hay for the goats to eat and straw for their bedding.

When you get back, you find Uncle Six standing at the bottom of the stairs, his expression perplexed.

You see the problem. He's put eight water barrels in the hold, but there's nowhere on the floor of the hold to put the ninth barrel, except inside the goats' pen. "Could we stack the last water barrel on top of the others?" you ask.

"We could…" he answers.

"But?" you ask.

"But will there be enough room for the 18 barrels of food?" he says.

"Each layer holds eight barrels," you say.

"We need 27 barrels all together. Eight barrels in one layer, 16 barrels in two layers, 24 barrels in three layers. We need to stack the barrels at least four high to fit all the barrels."

"Do you think the hold is tall enough?" he asks.

"Hmm..." You notice something. "The barrels are basically the same height as your legs, Uncle Six. They go up to your hip."

"Oh, smart!" he exclaims. He stands next to a barrel. "One barrel." He jumps up on top of the barrel and puts his hand palm down beside his hip. "Two barrels." Uncle Six is a great acrobat and very flexible. Standing on one leg, he kicks the other straight up, so his foot's above his head. There are only a few inches between his foot and the ceiling. "Three barrels," he says.

"We're only going to be able to stack the barrels three high," you say with a sigh. "That's only 24 barrels. That's three less than we need."

"We could put a stack of three barrels in the goat pen," he says.

"Then the goats will have less space than they need," you answer.

"Only a little..." he breaks off. "Or you could trade the crews' bunks out for hammocks."

"Trade out the bunks?" you ask.

"Yes!" he says, "Hammocks take up less space."

"Won't that be expensive?" you ask.

"A little expensive, but you may be able to sell the bunks, and the hammocks will save a lot of space," he says.

"So it'll take some money and it'll take some time and effort," you say. "Pirates are supposed to be efficient, and they're supposed to be thrifty."

"True," he says. "They also should take

good care of their animals."

"True," you answer.

"So, what do you want to do?" he asks.

Will you keep the bunks and stack three barrels in the goats' stall (turn to page 181)?

or

Will you buy hammocks to replace the bunks (turn to page 173)?

You're back on the farm with Aunt Farmer, and this time you're going to make a different choice. You choose five hens.

YOU CHOOSE CHICKENS

You choose the chickens. You know you need to save as much space as possible for provisions. Though the goats are cute and fun, they just take up too much room. Plus, you love a nice fried egg for breakfast.

The five chickens are all hens, of course. Berlinda is a petite chicken that Aunt Farmer tells you is prone to get chilly. Merlinda's tail feathers are sea green. Gerlinda's clucking has an unusually deep growling sound to it. Perlinda's white feathers are shiny like pearls. Ferlinda's feathers are so fluffy that she almost looks furry. All five are healthy birds and good layers.

You borrow a small wagon and cage to transport the birds to the ship. You walk slowly through Pirate Town, careful about where you steer the wagon, not wanting to jostle the hens. Aunt Farmer got them into the cage easily enough, but they seem to prefer her over you, and they aren't particularly adventurous. Every time you glance back at the wagon, you see them eyeing you suspiciously, their heads turned sideways to look at you.

During one of these glances back, you see something that catches your attention, a flash of red feathers in the crowd, like a parrot sitting on someone's shoulder. The streets are busy, and whatever you saw quickly disappears behind the crowd. Maybe it was nothing, but you've learned to keep an eye out for that sneaky pirate, Percival, and his parrot, Pamela. He might try to steal your chickens.

You walk backwards so you can pull the wagon while keeping an eye on the chickens. You look behind yourself frequently to see where you're going, but you still bump into a few surly pirates along the way. You apologize to each person you collide with and make it to the ship with no major incidents. You pull the wagon up the gangplank, and your chickens are safely aboard ship.

"Hello, Patrick," Uncle Six says. "Hello Lindas," he says to the birds.

They ignore him.

"Chickens are practical animals to have

aboard ship, and fresh eggs are mighty tasty. Good choice," he says to you.

"Thank you," you answer. "I have to decide whether to build them a coop up on deck or down in the hold."

"A chicken coop for five chickens doesn't take up much space," he says. "If you build it in the hold, you should still have plenty of room for provisions."

You nod.

He goes on. "Of course, if you build it up here, you would have even more space below. We could take some extra comforts with us on our voyage."

"Like what?" you ask.

He scratched his beard. "Well, a table and chairs on a long voyage is a mighty fine thing, a place where we can all sit together. Course, it isn't necessary. We can all eat together sitting on the floor, or the bunks, or up here on deck, but it is nice to sit down all civilized and have a meal."

"Hmm, that sounds nice," you answer. "Can we afford to buy a table and chairs?"

"We don't need to buy them," he answers. "I know someone who will lend them to us for free."

"Wow, that sounds really nice," you say.

"On the other hand," he says. "It's hard to build a coop tight enough that it doesn't leak and get the birds wet in a storm. There's a lot more water sloshing around on a ship's deck than on land, so you have to do a good job on the coop."

"Getting all wet isn't very nice for the chickens," you say, "and probably not very healthy for them either."

"No," he says, "and if a storm is big

enough, a wave might wash the coop right overboard and into the sea."

"How likely are we to meet a storm that big?" you ask.

"Not very likely," he answers, "In all probability, the chickens will be just fine on deck, but there's a slight chance they may not be. What do you want to do?"

Will you build the coop on deck so you have space for a table and chairs in the hold
(turn to page 153)?

or

Will you build the coop in the hold
(turn to page 166)?

You're back on the deck of the Barnacle Bucket with Uncle Six and the chickens. This time you're going to make a different choice. You choose to build the coop on deck.

YOU BUILD THE COOP ON THE DECK

You decide to build the coop on deck. Like Uncle Six said, the risk to the birds is small. You've been a cabin boy, and know that long sea voyages are a lot merrier if there is a comfortable place for everyone to gather and eat in the hold, so you're excited to get a table and chairs.

While you construct the coop, Uncle Six offers to pick up the furniture.

"Who will you borrow them from?" you ask.

"Grandpa Pirate," he answers with a wink.

"Grandpa Pirate!" you exclaim. "You don't mean the table and chairs in his dining room, do you?"

"That's exactly what I mean," he says.

"Oh, dear." Grandpa Pirate has a formal dining room with a beautiful oak table and chairs padded with green velvet. Grandpa Pirate rarely, if ever, uses the dining room, preferring to entertain guests in the parlor, but that doesn't mean he'll let you load his beautiful table and chairs into the Barnacle Bucket. What if the table is banged by a loose barrel and damaged? What if you have a shipwreck and the table ends up at the bottom of the sea? Would he ever let you captain the Pickled Pearl then? You're having serious second thoughts.

"Don't worry about it," Uncle Six says. "He's been talking about clearing out that room to make a sword fighting space. I'm sure he'll let us take it."

"That table is more valuable than anything else on the ship," you say.

"Hmm, I guess that's true," he says and smiles. "At least until we find the treasure." He springs down the gangplank and is gone.

You get to work on the chicken coop.

It's two feet wide and five feet long, 10 square feet total, with a nest box for each bird filled with straw. It has a small door for the chickens, which you can latch to keep them inside at night or in bad weather. The roof is removable for easy cleaning.

You stand up and take a step back to appreciate your work. That is one nice chicken coop. Your heart swells with pride.

You transfer the birds to the coop and then take the wagon and cage Aunt Farmer lent you back to the farm.

On your way back to the ship, you meet Uncle Six driving a horse and cart loaded with Grandpa Pirate's table and chairs. You climb up and he gives you a ride. As Uncle Six stops the cart on the dock, you see something unexpected.

There's a man coming down the gangplank of the Barnacle Bucket. He's carrying a sack, which is squirming and jerking every which way, like he's got a dragon trapped inside. It's that sneaky scallywag, Percival the Pirate, and he's stealing your chickens.

"Scurvy dog! Scurvy dog!" cries Pamela

the Parrot, flying in circles high above.

She must be the lookout, because Percival immediately drops the sack and takes off running. The sack hits the gangplank and then topples into the sea. You jump off the cart, kick off your shoes, and dive in to save the Lindas.

The water is murky and the salt stings your eyes, but the sack sinks only slowly. Perhaps the birds' thrashing helps keep it afloat, or perhaps the air trapped in the sack makes it buoyant. Either way, you find it easily, grab hold, and Uncle Six throws you a line and pulls you from the water.

On the ship you find the coop you built broken, so you take the chickens down to the hold and let them out of the sack. They're very flustered but seem unharmed. You only have a moment to inspect the birds before Gerlinda attacks you. She beats you with her wings, jumps at you, scratches with her leg spurs and pecks you. It's lucky you're wearing thick pants. You run up the steps and close the trapdoor, trapping Gerlinda and the other hens below.

You sit down beside the broken coop, wet and panting. You roll up a pant leg to examine a scratch.

"She's just trying to protect herself and the other birds," Uncle Six says.

"I didn't put her in a sack and drop her in the ocean," you say.

He shrugs. "It's just instinct," he says. "She's frightened."

You nod. "They could have died. Percival nearly killed them."

"Poor Lindas," he says.

You and your uncle examine the wreckage of the coop. It would seem that Percival didn't realize that the top was removable, and unable to reach the birds through the small door, he pried up the boards, breaking some of them.

"I'm not sure this was waterproof to begin with," Uncle Six says. "While we repair it, we should make some improvements to make sure the birds stay dry in storms."

You feel humbled and far less proud of your workmanship on the coop and of your decision to build it on deck. "Let's just nail the boards back on, wait for the hens to calm down, and then move it into the hold," you say, "where they'll be safe, and we won't have to worry about it being waterproof."

He chuckles. "I think that's a good idea, but you should be the one to take the table and chairs back to Grandpa Pirate. I'll get our water barrels filled up and put them down in the hold. Then you can buy our provisions. We'll need 18 barrels of food"

You agree. "Be careful of Gerlinda when you take the water barrels down there," you say.

"I think that little hen will calm down soon, but don't worry. I spent my childhood helping Aunt Farmer with her farm while Grandpa Pirate was at sea. I know how to handle chickens."

You drive the wagon with the table and chairs back to Grandpa Pirate's house. As you enter the house, you hear the ringing of swords. Looking through the doorway into the dining room, you see Grandpa Pirate and Aunt Farmer engaged in an epic sword fight. They are both fantastic—parrying, thrusting, and pivoting with surprising speed and agility for two such old siblings, one of them a farmer.

The match is close, but Grandpa Pirate wins in the end. You're glad. He is the best pirate in the seven seas, after all. How would it look for him to lose a sword fight to a farmer? You think Aunt Farmer would have made an excellent pirate, but she loved caring for animals and she loved Uncle Farmer, so you think she made the right choice.

They shake hands, and, panting, they both turn and look at you.

"You bringing back my table?" Grandpa Pirate asks.

You nod. "How did you know?"

"That table's huge and that schooner is small," he says. "I figured you'd have trouble getting it through the trapdoor into the hold."

"Oh," you say, blushing. Of course, you never tried fitting it through the door, but you think he might be right, and you're embarrassed that that problem never occurred to you. Pirates need to be detail oriented. You should have measured the doorway.

"Why are you damp?" Aunt Farmer asks.

You tell them what happened.

"That sneaky pirate, Percival!" she exclaims. "Are the birds all right?"

You assure her they're fine.

After you get the table and chairs put back in Grandpa Pirate's dining room, you go back to the ship, repair the coop and move it into the hold. You shut the chickens in the coop for the night. None of them try to attack you, but Gerlinda still eyes you suspiciously. Even though you saved their lives, the birds don't consider you a friend yet. You wonder if they ever will.

It's too late now to buy the 18 barrels of provisions you need. You'll have to visit the merchant in the morning, so it will delay your journey a day. At least the birds are safe and you can expect fresh eggs on your trip. You head to bed.

Your choices here had mixed results. Everyone's okay, but the chickens were in serious danger, you looked silly in front of Grandpa Pirate, and your voyage is delayed a day.

This book has four different endings so if you haven't seen them all, you can:

Go back one step and build the coop in the

hold (turn to page 165).

Go back two steps and choose the goats instead of the chickens (turn to page 136).

Go back to the beginning and re-read the first scene (turn to page 127).

If you've read all four endings, then turn to page 189.

You're back on the deck of the Barnacle Bucket with Uncle Six and the chickens. This time you're going to make a different choice. You choose to build the coop in the hold.

YOU BUILD THE COOP IN THE HOLD

You decide to build the coop in the hold. The risk might be small, but it's not worth risking the chickens' lives to build their coop on deck just to save a few square feet in the hold. It would be nice to have a table and chairs, but it would take more time for Uncle Six to go get them, and you want to make sure that you can get the ship fully provisioned today. You plan to set sail bright and early tomorrow morning.

While you're building the coop, Uncle Six fills the water barrels and brings them down into the hold. There are nine of them and they fit with plenty of room to spare. The 18 food barrels you'll get will fit easily as well.

When you finish the coop, you take the chickens from their cage and set them inside it. Then you take the wagon and cage back to the farm.

When you get back to the dock, you see Percival the Pirate running down the gangplank of the Barnacle Bucket!

"Get back here, you mangy sneak!" Uncle Six yells as he chases after him.

You jump in front Percival, trying to stop him, but he just growls and pushes you to the side.

Arms flailing, you fall off the side of the dock and into the sea. The water is dark and murky. You break the surface, coughing and spluttering.

"Hold on! I'll get you a line!" Uncle Six shouts, and then he throws you a rope and pulls you from the water.

You sit on the dock rubbing your stinging eyes, coughing, and spitting out water.

Uncle Six pats your back. "That sneaky pirate..." he grumbles angrily.

"What was he doing on the ship?" you ask.

"I caught him sneaking around the deck, looking for things to steal," he says.

You have a sinking feeling in your stomach. "What did he take?"

"Nothing," Uncle Six says, and you feel a swell of relief. "There's nothing much on deck for him to steal."

"I'm glad I put the chickens down in the hold," you say.

"Me too," he answers, "and I'm glad you're okay."

The story of Percival the Pirate pushing you off the pier spreads quickly through Pirate Town. When you visit the merchant to buy the 18 barrels of food, he's heard the story and gives you a good deal on the provisions. You're able to buy the 18 barrels of beans, salted beef and fish, and hard tack sea biscuits at a great price, and you have a few coins left in your pouch. You and your uncle load the provisions into the hold. Everything is ready and you can set sail in the morning.

You walk to the mermaid cove to tell Marina and McCartney (who will serve as ship's navigator) that you sail in the morning.

The mermaids have a merry laugh at the story of your misadventure. "I have no idea why you land-legs try so hard to stay out of the sea. Being in the water is so much better than being on the land," McCartney says.

"I agree," you say, "but with one big difference. I think that being on the sea is better than being on land. There's nothing so fine as sailing on a ship."

The mermaids invite you to a dinner of fish and kelp. You eat hungrily and tell them it's one of the best meals you've ever had. Then you lay on the beach looking up at the stars, and you fall asleep and dream of adventure, and treasure, and tomorrow.

Your choices here worked out well. Falling into the ocean was dangerous, but that wasn't your fault and you're all right. You got a great deal on provisions, and you're ready to sail.

This book has four different endings so if you haven't seen them all, you can:

Go back one step and build the coop on the deck (turn to page 152).
Go back two steps and choose the goats instead of the chickens (turn to page 136).
Go back to the beginning and re-read the first scene (turn to page 127).
If you've read all four endings, turn to page 189.

You're back in the hold of the Barnacle Bucket with Uncle Six and the goats. This time you're going to make a different choice. You choose to replace the bunks with hammocks.

YOU REPLACE THE BUNKS WITH HAMMOCKS

You decide to trade the bunks for hammocks.

You're far from sure that this is the right decision. You worry about the comfort of the crew. What if people can't sleep in the hammocks? There's no one grumpier than a grumpy pirate; a ship full of them would be unpleasant. However, Aunt Farmer told you how much room the goats would need and you promised to take good care of them. You have to free up space in the hold, and hammocks save space.

The hammock seller is a short man with a peg leg who works out of a cart near the dock. You ask him if he'll accept the ship's bunks in exchange for hammocks.

He laughs like that's the funniest thing he ever heard. "What on Earth would I want with bunks? Hammocks are the future. In just a few years, every ship will have hammocks. You can't beat the comfort of a hammock at sea."

You eye the hammocks in the cart doubtfully. They're made from knotted rope and don't look comfortable in the least. You imagine waking up each morning with crisscrossing rope imprints on your skin. You'd rather stick with bunks, but you don't have the space. "Can you give me any suggestions about who might be interested in buying the bunks?" you ask.

The man taps his chin. "Bunks are no good at sea, but they work well enough on land," he says. "You might check with Granny Smith, who runs the boarding house. I heard she was thinking of putting in some new beds."

"Thank you," you say. "I'll be back."

The boarding house is a busy place, and Granny Smith is a busy woman. Pirate Town is a busy port and there aren't enough beds for all the people, pirate or otherwise, who come ashore for a brief stay. Standing in the parlor of the boarding house, you can't imagine that she needs more bunks, since the place is already jam-packed with them. You ask her, anyway.

"Sure," she says. "I could use some more bunks."

You look around in disbelief. The parlor

contains as many bunks as it can hold. You can't imagine that the bedrooms are any different.

She chuckles. "I've still got some space in the kitchen. Bring me the bunks and I'll buy them."

So you do, and you use her money to buy the hammocks.

"You're making the right choice," the hammock seller tells you.

"I hope so," you answer.

"They're great for seasickness," he says.

"They are?" you ask. "Why would that be?"

"Because they hang and aren't stuck the way bunks are. As the ship moves, the hammocks stay relatively still," he answers.

"Wow," you say, and for the first time you're a little excited about this hammock idea.

Uncle Six helps you hang them and he

sticks his mattress onto his hammock, so you do the same and you both try them out. The first time you climb into your hammock, you flip right out the other side onto the floor of the hold, but the second time you make it in. You're just going to have to be careful until you get used to it.

With your bedding in it, the hammock is remarkably comfortable, probably even more so than the bunks were. You smile as you start to drift off to sleep. *Now's not the time!* you tell yourself. You still need to buy provisions if you're going to sail tomorrow. You sit bolt upright and again the hammock flips and dumps you on the floor. This is going to take some getting used to.

You buy 18 barrels of beans, salted beef and fish, and hard tack sea biscuits for a fair price from the merchant. You spend almost all the money in your pouch, but you have everything you need to sail tomorrow. Uncle Six helps you load all the barrels into the hold. You stack them three high.

You go to the Mermaid Cove to let Marina and McCartney (the navigator) know that you'll be sailing tomorrow. You eat a meal of fish and kelp with them and then go back to the ship. You check on the goats, pet their heads, and wish them goodnight. Then you get into your hammock. You're so excited about tomorrow that you worry you won't be able to sleep, but it's so comfortable that you're out in no time.

Your choices worked well here. Your goats are happy and healthy. You have all the food and water your ship needs. You bought hammocks which save space, are comfortable, and prevent sea sickness (though they can be a little tricky to use.)

This book has four different endings so if you haven't seen them all, you can:

Go back one step and keep the bunks (turn to page 180).
Go back two steps and choose the chickens instead of the goats (turn to page 145).
Go back to the beginning and re-read the first scene (turn to page 127).
If you've read all four endings, turn to page 189.

You're back in the hold of the Barnacle Bucket with Uncle Six and the goats. This time you're going to make a different choice. You choose to keep the bunks and stack three barrels in the goats' stall.

YOU KEEP THE BUNKS

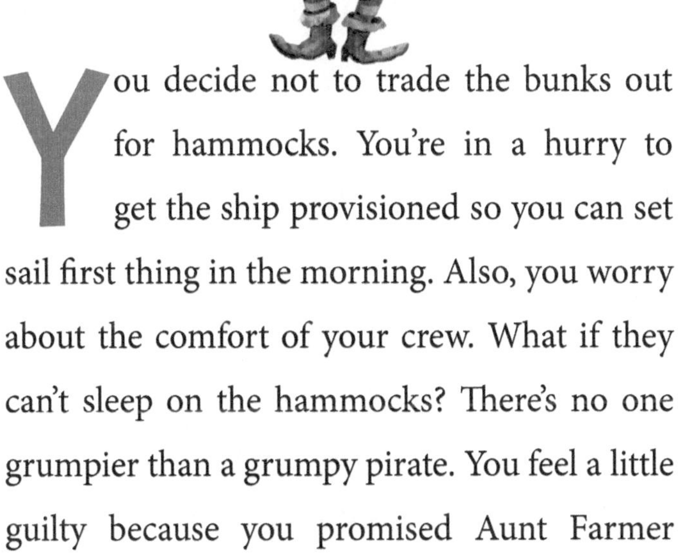

You decide not to trade the bunks out for hammocks. You're in a hurry to get the ship provisioned so you can set sail first thing in the morning. Also, you worry about the comfort of your crew. What if they can't sleep on the hammocks? There's no one grumpier than a grumpy pirate. You feel a little guilty because you promised Aunt Farmer you'd take good care of the animals, and you're not giving the goats all the space she said they would need, but it's a small difference and it's temporary. Once you've eaten the food in a few of the barrels, you can move them out to give the goats more room.

You go to the merchant and buy the 16 barrels of food you need. You get a fair price on beans, salted beef and fish, and hardtack sea biscuits. It costs almost all the money you have in your pouch, but you now have everything you need for the voyage.

In the hold, you stack the 27 barrels three high (nine barrels contain water and 18 contain food.) One stack of three is inside the goats' stall.

You're ready to set sail! You can embark first thing in the morning. You're so excited. You and Uncle Six get meat pies at a food stand in

Pirate Town to celebrate. They're hot, delicious, and filled with a rich gravy. *This is the life!* you think. There's nothing better than being a pirate captain about to set sail on a ship, even if that ship is the Barnacle Bucket.

When you get back to the Bucket, you go down into the hold planning to get a good night's sleep, but you're met with an awful smell. The odor practically singes the inside of your nose, it's so rank. You've never smelled anything like it, and you live in Pirate Town, a place not known for its pleasant aromas.

As you get to the bottom of the stairs, Daisy lets out a gigantic fart. A moment later, Midnight does the same. Daisy gives a mournful sound, her head and ears drooping. The goats' stomachs look swollen and fat.

"Oh, no!" you say, seeing the source of the problem. The goats have knocked down the stack of barrels in their stall and one of the barrels broke open, spilling out the beans inside. The goats have been gorging themselves on the beans.

Uncle Six takes one look (and whiff) and hurries back up the stairs. "I'll get Aunt Farmer!" he calls.

Plugging your nose, you pet the goats and try to comfort them. All the while, they're farting, burping, and moaning. They're miserable and they've made themselves sick, but you're the one who's to blame. You should have gotten the hammocks instead of putting those three barrels in their stall. You're lucky they weren't injured when they knocked them over.

When Aunt Farmer arrives, she croons to the goats and pets them. Then she lifts Midnight and carries her up the stairs, off the ship, and to the cart she has waiting on the dock. She does the same with Daisy. You follow her, your head hanging, to the cart. "I'm so sorry, Aunt Farmer," you say.

She nods, her lips a tight line. "I told you how much space they need."

"I know, Aunt Farmer," you say. "I'm sorry."

She nods again. "I think these girls will recover just fine, but I'm taking them back to the farm to watch over them. You won't have any animals on your voyage."

"Yes, ma'am," you answer sadly. "Of course, with those beans gone, we don't have enough provisions for the journey. I'll have to postpone until I can earn some money to buy more."

"I saw you bought the goats some nice fresh hay," she says. "That's one thing you got right."

"Yes, ma'am," you answer.

She sighs, but then smiles. "I'll buy the hay from you so you can replace the beans," she says.

"Thank you, ma'am," you say, and hurry to get the hay.

The merchant is closed, so you have to wait until the next morning to buy a new barrel of beans. You miss the tide, so you have to wait another day to start on your voyage.

You go by the farm to visit the goats. They seem to be feeling quite a bit better. You'll miss them on the voyage and you'll miss having their milk, but you're still excited to set sail.

Your choices turned out poorly. The goats got sick and they could have been injured because you didn't give them enough living space. You won't have any animals (or the fresh food they provide) on your journey. You're delayed a day before you can set sail.

This book has four different endings so if you haven't seen them all, you can:

Go back one step and replace the bunks with hammocks (turn to page 172).
Go back two steps and choose the chickens instead of the goats (turn to page 145).
Go back to the beginning and re-read the first scene (turn to page 127).
If you've read all four endings, turn to page 189.

MATH PIRATES
TREASURE HUNT

S.E. BURR

TREASURE MAP

TREASURE HUNT

The crew of the Barnacle Bucket includes six members.

First, there's you, Patrick the Pirate, ship's captain.

Then there are the two mermaids, Marina, your best friend, and McCartney. McCartney is your cousin, she's eighteen years old, she's a mermaid, and she's going to serve as ship's navigator on your voyage. Her father is your uncle, Wade. McCartney's mother and Marina's mother are sisters. So, both you and Marina are McCartney's cousins, but you're not related to each other at all. You're just good friends.

Uncle Six is first mate. He's bald, muscular and exactly six feet tall.

Uncle Wade, McCartney's father, is the helmsman. He steers the ship. He wears a black hat, a fashionable striped shirt, and brown waders—waterproof overalls that let him wade in waist high water without getting wet. He really enjoys wading, and that's why he's called Uncle Wade.

Dr. Fish, Marina's father, is both ship's doctor and ship's cook. He's a tall man who wears fish scale pants.

The journey to the island is pleasant.

There's nothing in the world you like more than sailing. This is the life for you.

One morning after you've been at sea for a few days, you wake early, throw off your blanket, and climb the stairs two at a time, excited to face the day. On deck, you find Uncle Wade, who's on watch, standing at the stern and looking out to sea with a spyglass. You walk over and stand beside him.

He hands you the spyglass. "Take a look," he says.

You do, and at first you see nothing but empty sea and sky, but then you spot something—a distant speck on the horizon. Perhaps it's just a reflection off the water? But you don't think so. "What is it?" you ask.

"A ship," he answers. "We're being followed."

You take a deep breath and then bend

down and give two sharp tugs on the two ropes dangling off the back of the ship.

You and Uncle Wade back away to give the mermaids the space they need. A moment passes and then McCartney leaps from the water and onto the deck. A few seconds later, Marina does the same. They each untie the rope from around their waist. The mermaids prefer to sleep in the water. They tie themselves to the ship so they don't get left behind.

"Good morning, ladies," you say. "Sorry to wake you, but we need to put on some speed." You glance at Uncle Wade out of the corner of your eye. Technically, you're in command of the ship, but Uncle Wade is the more experienced pirate.

He nods in approval. "I'll wake the others," he says.

You sail the ship as fast as you can, but the speck is still there. You can't outrun it.

At local noon, meaning the time when the sun is highest in the sky, McCartney uses her sextant to calculate the ship's position. Local noon is rarely if ever actually 12 o'clock. She uses the mirrors on the sextant to make it appear as though the sun were resting on the horizon and then writes down the time and the angle shown on the sextant. She consults her nautical charts to find your latitude. Latitude is the ship's North / South position. Finding the longitude, the ship's East / West position, requires a more complex calculation, using the sextant to site the moon.

After she's taken your position, the crew sits down together to eat lunch and to discuss the situation.

"We can expect to reach the island

tomorrow," McCartney says.

"We should decide what to do about Percival the Pirate before we get there," you say.

"Are we even sure that it's Percival's ship?" asks Marina. "Maybe it's someone else, or maybe it's just a coincidence that a ship is behind us, and we're not being followed at all."

"Maybe," you say, "but I think it's him. Percival, his daughter Becky, and their parrot Pamela will stop at nothing to get the treasure."

"I agree," says Uncle Six. "Maybe it's not Percival, but it seems too much to hope for that he has given up. I think we need to assume it's him and make a plan to get the treasure and to keep that troublesome trio away from it."

The crew nods.

"Does anyone have any ideas?" you ask.

"I have an idea," says McCartney. "When we near the island, Marina and I will jump overboard and swim to the beach. Meanwhile, the Barnacle Bucket will keep right on sailing, and Percival will think we are just passing by the island on our way to find the treasure somewhere else. You'll sail on for a day or so and then turn back. When we see the ship, we'll swim out with the treasure. You'll pick us up, and then we'll speed back to Pirate Town as quick as we can."

"But how will you get the treasure?" you ask. "It's not on the beach. You'd have to walk to it."

McCartney smiles. "Tomorrow night is the full moon."

"Oh," you say. On the full moon, mermaids' fins turn to legs. "Will you be able to find the treasure at night?"

"No problem," says Marina. "The moon will be full, and besides, we can see in the dark."

"But will you be able to swim out with the treasure?" you ask. "It might be really heavy."

Marina just raises an eyebrow. McCartney scowls at you.

Dr. Fish laughs. "Don't go questioning mermaid abilities, son," he says. "There's nothing stronger than them in the water. Why, Marina's mother fought a great white shark barehanded once, and she won."

Your eyes widen in surprise. "Wow," is all you can say.

Marina gives a pleased smile.

You think of another problem with the plan. "What if we can't find our way back to the island? You're our navigator," you say to McCartney. Around you, the other crew members frown. It would be awful if you got lost and left Marina and McCartney stranded on the island.

McCartney shrugs. "Just keep sailing straight and then sail straight back the other way. The winds have been calm. You'll be able to find the island again easily enough."

"If you say so," you answer. "Any other ideas?" you ask the crew.

"I have an idea," says Uncle Wade. He points to the treasure map. "We'll steer the ship into this bay at the river mouth by Skull Rock. Dr. Fish will row you and Six to shore. Then he'll bring back the rowboat."

"That bay is really far from the treasure," Uncle Six says.

"Exactly!" Says Uncle Wade. "Percival is a pirate, not a tracker. He'll have a much harder time following you on land than on water. You'll walk across the island to find the treasure. Meanwhile, we'll sail the ship around the other side of the island and pick you up here." He points to the northern shore near the X.

"Hmm," you say. "How are we for water?" you ask. "We were planning to refill our empty water barrels at the island. Neither plan allows us time for that."

"We have plenty of water left for the voyage home," says Dr. Fish. "We don't need to refill them."

"What do you want to do, captain?" Uncle Six asks.

Will you send McCartney and Marina to get the treasure (turn to page 204)?

or

Will you and Uncle Six cross the island to get the treasure (turn to page 216)?

You're back on the Barnacle Bucket deciding on a plan to get the treasure. This time you choose McCartney's plan.

MCCARTNEY'S PLAN

You worry about your friends being alone on the island. What if there's some unknown danger, like wild beasts or bottomless pits? What if you have a hard time getting back to the island and you leave them for longer than you agreed? As captain, you prefer to take on the danger yourself, but this plan is both clever and sneaky. Percival the Pirate, his daughter Becky, and their parrot Pamela are brilliant, sneaky pirates. You need to be as clever and as sneaky as possible in order to beat them to the treasure.

Sitting on the deck and looking at the treasure map of the island, you work out the details of the plan with the mermaids.

"We'll approach the island from the east," McCartney says. "With a spyglass, we may or may not see the rusty anchor, but we should be able to see the hills on the eastern side of the island. We'll turn the ship to starboard…"

"To the right," Marina supplies.

"Right, right," McCartney says. "I mean, correct, we'll turn the ship to the right and sail along the northern coast of the island. We'll see the smaller island beside the bigger one. As we get close to the small island, Marina and I will jump into the water on the port side, the left side, of the ship and swim toward that little piece of land north of the X that juts out into the sea."

"Would that be called a headland, or a cape, or a point?" Marina asks.

McCartney takes a long look at the map. "It doesn't really look enough like a peninsula to be any of those. It's not mostly surrounded by water. It's just a little piece of shore that sticks further into the water than the shore beside it. Because it sticks out into the water, we won't have to swim as far."

"All right," says Marina. "How far from the shore is the treasure?"

You cut a little piece of string to be the same length as the scale marked on the map. The scale shows that that length on the map equals 1,000 paces in real life. The center of the X is about two string lengths from the shore.

"About 2,000 paces," you say.

"Whose paces?" Marina asks.

You tap your chin, thinking. "Grandpa Pirate's, I suppose."

"How long is a pace?" Marina asks.

"Hmm," you say. You look at the two mermaids, imagining them with legs instead of fins. You've seen them with legs before, having attended some of the full moon dances they host in mermaid cove. "McCartney, I think you're about the same height as Grandpa Pirate, so your steps would be about the same. You count 2,000 paces from the shore and that should be about where the treasure is."

"Do you think it will be easy to find?" McCartney asks. "I'd hate to have to dig a bunch of holes."

"I think Grandpa Pirate probably marked the spot, maybe with an X on the ground, or maybe it won't even be buried," you say. "This is a quest to prove I'm ready to be a pirate captain. I think sailing to the island and following the map to the treasure are what he's testing, not digging…"

"You think," says McCartney.

"I think," you repeat, "but I could be wrong."

She nods. "Fair enough."

You continue to discuss the plan. "After you two have left the ship, we'll keep sailing westward around the northern side of the island," you say. "Maybe we'll take this channel between the big island and the smaller one?"

"I wouldn't recommend it," says McCartney. "It might be shallow or rocky. You don't want to run aground."

"All right, so we'll go around the little island and then we'll follow the western shore south, past the sand dunes until we get to the inlet on the western shore," you say. "Then we'll turn starboard, right, and start sailing west again."

"And hopefully Percival the Pirate will think you're sailing to something to the west, and you simply had to take a small detour to get around the island," says McCartney.

The next day you enact the plan, and at first it goes off without a hitch. Approaching the island from the east, you can see the rusty anchor and the hills through your spyglass. You turn starboard and sail around the north edge of the island where the mermaids jump off the ship and swim to shore. You continue sailing around the west side of the island where you see the sand dunes and the inlet. You can also see the side of Skull Rock in the distance.

You turn starboard again and continue sailing west. The other ship continues to follow you. You continue sailing west for the rest of that day and into the night.

But then things go terribly wrong. An awful storm kicks up, tossing the ship every which way, and monster waves crash over the sides. You're glad you don't have a chicken coop on deck like some ships do, because if you did, the poor hens would have been washed into the sea within the first half hour of the storm. Your crew is made up of excellent sailors, and you make it through the storm with the ship intact and no one injured, but as the morning dawns, you realize you have no idea where you are. You were supposed to continue straight west from the island, so that you could turn around and head straight east back to it. You don't know where the storm has driven you, but you're sure it's off your intended course. You turn east now to head back toward the island, but you're worried that it may take days to find it.

In the distance you see a white flag and head to it. You find Percival, Becky, and Pamela in a rowboat, the wreckage of what had been their ship floating in the water around them.

You haul them aboard.

"Thanks for the rescue," says Percival.

"Thanks," says Becky.

"Scallywags!" says the parrot.

Becky looks around the deck of your ship. "Where are the mermaids?" she asks.

When you don't answer immediately, Percival's eyes widen and then he gives a knowing grin. "They're back there on that island we passed, aren't they? Retrieving the treasure, I bet." He laughs. "That is a sneaky trick."

"Thanks," you say.

"But you don't know how to get back to the island now, do you?" Becky asks. "Not after that storm. McCartney was your navigator."

You hesitate, but what's the harm in telling them? They're shipwrecked. You've saved them. They have no chance of taking the treasure now.

You nod. "We'll just have to look until we find it," you say.

"Maybe not," says Percival. He squeezes Becky's shoulder. "My daughter is an excellent navigator. She can help you find your way to the island, to the treasure, and to your mermaid friends."

"You can?" you ask Becky.

Before answering, she reaches into her bag and pulls out a sextant, holding it up for you to see. "Sure," she says.

"Great!" you say.

"If you give us each a share of the treasure," she says.

"What!" you say. "But we saved your lives. You're on our ship! We could put you right back in that row boat and let you fend for yourselves on the open ocean!"

"You could," she agrees, "but you won't."

She's right. You won't. You may be a pirate, but you're not a bad guy. "You want two shares of the treasure?" you ask.

"Three," Percival says.

"Three?" you ask.

"One for me, one for Becky, and one for Pamela," he answers.

"Your parrot gets a share!" you exclaim.

"If you accept Becky's help, I'll give up my share," says Dr. Fish. "That way the treasure will be divided into eight shares rather than nine. I'm just anxious to get back to my little girl."

"How about it?" asks Becky.

The entire crew, along with the three new passengers, look at you expectantly.

Will you ask Becky to help you find the way back to the island for three shares of the treasure? The treasure will be divided into eight shares, because Dr. Fish has offered to give up his share. (Turn to page 245.)

or

Will you try to find the island without Becky's help? The treasure will be divided into six shares. (Turn to page 253.)

You're back on the Barnacle Bucket deciding on a plan to get the treasure. This time you choose Uncle Wade's plan.

UNCLE WADE'S PLAN

As the ship's captain, you would rather take a risk yourself than put your friends in danger. You don't know if there is anything dangerous on the island, but if there is, you will be the one to face it.

You sit on the deck with Uncle Six and McCartney and make a plan.

"We will approach the island from the

east," says McCartney. "We should be able to see those hills on the eastern shore with a spyglass."

"What about the rusty anchor?" you ask.

"Maybe, maybe not," she answers.

"Being able to see two different landmarks at once helps you know where you are on a map," you say.

"Right," says Uncle Six, "and so does a shoreline and a compass. It doesn't matter exactly where we are as we approach the eastern coast, because we will not put ashore there. We're going to sail around to the southern coast."

"Correct," says McCartney. "We'll approach the island from the east. Then we'll turn the ship to port(left) and sail south around the southern tip of the island. We'll turn again, this time to starboard (right), and sail into the bay on the southern side of the island. Then you two will get in the rowboat and Dr. Fish will row you to shore. You'll put ashore between the river mouth and Skull Rock. Those are the two landmarks that will let you know where you are on the map."

"Then we'll walk from the shore to where the X is on the map and find the treasure," you say.

"How far is it from the shore to the X?" Uncle Six asks.

You cut a string to be the same length as the scale marked on the map. That distance on the map means 1,000 paces in real life. From the shore to the center of the X is four string lengths. "About 4,000 paces," you say.

"Who's paces?" McCartney asks.

"Probably Grandpa Pirate's," says Uncle Six and frowns. "I'm a little taller than him, so my steps are probably longer than his. You're a lot shorter than him, Patrick, so your steps are probably shorter than his."

"Hmm," you say. "You're a little taller than him, so maybe just take steps that are a little shorter than normal."

He shrugs. "All right. As we're walking, we should be able to see the river to our right and the sand dunes to our left. That's how we'll know we're on the right track."

"And if we get to the northern shore of the island, we'll know we've gone too far," you finish.

"While you're doing that, Dr. Fish will row back out to the Barnacle Bucket and we'll hoist the row boat and him back aboard," says McCartney. "Then we'll sail around the island to meet you on the north shore when you have the treasure."

"Sounds good," you say, and the others

nod.

The next day you enact the plan, and it starts out well. The Barnacle Bucket approaches the island from the east. Using the spyglass. You look straight ahead and see the expected hills. A little to the right, you can see the rusty anchor, too.

Uncle Wade turns the ship to port (to the left) and you sail around the southern tip of the island. You give a wide smile as Skull Rock comes into view.

Dr. Fish rows you and Uncle Six to shore, and that's when the first unexpected thing happens. Instead of turning the rowboat around and heading back to the Barnacle Bucket, Dr. Fish jumps from the boat and pulls it up on shore.

"What are you doing?" you ask.

He doesn't answer. Instead, he strides

forward and examines a tall tree with large leaves and small pink blossoms. "This is a cinchona tree!" he exclaims.

"What?" you ask.

"This tree is medicine!" he says. "The bark of the cinchona tree is what quinine is made from."

"What?" you ask again.

"Quinine is used to treat deadly malaria," Uncle Six says, sounding excited.

Dr. Fish pulls a knife from his belt and begins harvesting the bark from the tree.

"That's great," you say, "but you need to get back to the ship, so you can sail around the island and pick us up when we get the treasure."

"No problem," Dr. Fish says, continuing to cut off bark. "4,000 steps to the treasure, right? That's around two miles. Then another, what? 2,000 steps to the shore while carrying a heavy treasure? I'll harvest this tree and we'll have plenty of time to get to the northern shore to meet you."

"Are you sure?" you ask.

"Sure," he answers, but he doesn't sound sure. He turns briefly and looks at you. "Tell you what, I'll give up my share of the treasure. You can divide it into five shares instead of six. I found my treasure right here," he says, indicating the tree.

"All right," you say, reluctantly agreeing, and you and Uncle Six walk away.

It's a tough walk. The land between the river and the sand dunes is marshy and wet. With each step you take, you have to pull your foot from the mud with a squelch. It's a terrible trudge. Dr. Fish is probably right that he has plenty of time to harvest the quinine before picking you up.

When you've gone about 3,000 exhausting paces, the ground ahead of you looks dry. You see a lovely path of golden sand stretching before you. You and Uncle Six hurry forward and fall into quicksand!

The way the tales tell it, many intrepid young adventurers have met their ends sinking beneath the sands of this particular peril. It's a good story, but not a true one. It's very difficult to drown in quicksand. You and Uncle Six are too buoyant to completely sink, and you can easily keep your heads above the surface.

You won't drown, but you may not get out soon, either. The field of quicksand is huge and there's nothing solid to grab onto anywhere, and you and Uncle Six were already tired out when you fell in.

After at least an hour of struggle, you hear squelching footsteps. "Help!" you and

Uncle Six shout.

The steps get closer and then there's a laugh. "Well Pamela, look at the pickle these two are in," says Percival the Pirate.

"Pickle!" the parrot repeats.

"Are you two all right?" asks Becky.

If it had been members of your crew who found you instead of this tricky trio, you would have asked them for help immediately, but you say, "We're doing just fine, thank you."

Percival laughs again. "Oh, are you?"

"Yes, indeed," you answer.

"You don't reckon you need a little help?" Becky asks. "We've got a long rope. We could pull you from that perilous pit, no problem."

You hesitate. "What will it cost us?" you ask.

"Why, not so much," says Percival, "just one share of your treasure."

"One share?" you repeat.

"Yes, just one for each of us, one for me, one for Becky, and one for Pamela," he says.

"You want a share for your parrot!" you exclaim.

"Yes indeed," he says. "So, what do you say?"

You look at Uncle Six. "It's up to you," he says.

Will you ask Percival, Becky, and Pamela to pull you out of the quicksand for three shares of treasure (turn to page 227)?

or

Will you continue trying to get out of the quicksand on your own (turn to page 236)?

You and Uncle Six are back in the quicksand and this time you're going to ask Percival, Becky, and Pamela to pull you out.

ASK FOR HELP OUT OF THE QUICKSAND

You decide to ask for their help in exchange for shares of the treasure. Dividing the treasure into eight shares instead of five means that you and each member of your crew will get a lot less treasure. For instance, if the treasure contains 80 gold coins and you divide it into five shares, you each get 16 coins, because 80 divided by five is

16. However, if you divide 80 coins into eight shares, you each only get 10 coins. That's a big difference, but if you don't ask for their help, you might be stuck in the quicksand for a long time, and what if they find the treasure on their own? They don't have the map, but if they keep walking in the direction you were going before you got stuck, they might find it. You don't know if it's buried, well-hidden, or sitting out in plain sight. You just know where the X is on the map.

"All right," you say. "Pull us out, and you can each have a share of the treasure, all three of you." It's ridiculous that the parrot gets a share, but what can you do? Your only other choice is to stay in the quicksand.

They toss you one end of a long rope and Percival and Becky haul on the other end to pull you and Uncle Six from the quicksand. Pamela doesn't help. That parrot doesn't deserve part of the treasure! Oh well…

Past the quicksand, the path quickly becomes drier and easier to walk. Uncle Six forgot how many paces he walked before the two of you fell in. You think you may have to walk to the shore and then count 2,000 paces back, but that turns out not to be necessary. You easily find the not-very-well-hidden treasure chest beneath a few branches. You're glad you offered them the shares in exchange for pulling you out. If you hadn't, they might have found the treasure while you were still stuck in the sand.

You open the lid to reveal shiny gold bars. "Wow," you say. "I thought it would be coins."

Percival scowls, "So did I. How are we going to divide that evenly? he asks. "They'll have to be cut into pieces, so we all get equal shares."

"All right," you answer. "We'll cut them into pieces, then."

"You got a tool for cutting gold on your ship?" Becky asks.

"No," you answer. "Do you?"

"No." she says.

At that, Percival takes the bars from the chest one at a time and counts them. "I'll write up a receipt of how many bars there are, and that you owe each of us a one-eighth share, and then and we can both sign it."

Uncle Six elbows you, "Better make it two receipts," he whispers.

"Draw up two receipts," you tell Percival. "You'll have a copy, and we'll have a copy."

He writes up the receipts and you both sign each of them. "Now I'll take this here gold back to Pirate Town," says Percival, "and get it cut up and divided."

Uncle Six elbows you again, but you don't need his prompting this time. "No," you say. "*We'll* take the gold back to Pirate Town and get it cut up and divided."

Percival scowls again.

"All right," says Becky. "The gold will sail to Pirate Town on Patrick's ship."

"Nay," says her father. "That's madness."

"Nay," says Becky. "It's not. There are three reasons that they should take it back to Pirate Town. First, their crew is bigger than ours, which will come in handy in case sneaky pirates attack."

You stifle a laugh. In your opinion, sneaky pirates are already making off with three shares of the treasure, more if you let them.

Becky goes on. "Second, our ship is faster. We can follow them anywhere. They wouldn't be able to escape us even if they tried. Third, they won't try. Patrick is an honest pirate, if ever I've seen one."

Percival gasps. "An honest pirate!"

"Aye," Becky answers.

"I suppose he has that honest look about him," Percival says. "All right, aye. You take the treasure back to Pirate Town and we'll divide the treasure there. But mind, we'll be following you the entire way. Don't try anything funny."

"Of course not," you say. Then you and Uncle Six carry the treasure to the beach where Dr. Fish is waiting to pick you up in the rowboat. He was right. He did have plenty of time to harvest the quinine. He rows you to the Barnacle Bucket. You immediately set sail for Pirate Town. That evening you have a celebration on board with extra rations and beautiful music. The mermaids are talented singers. Their voices are so lovely, they could make a pirate captain shed a happy tear. Only when no other pirates are looking, mind.

Your decisions worked out well. You've got the treasure, and you're headed home. You've completed Grandpa Pirate's quest, and you'll soon be captain of the Pickled Pearl, the best pirate ship in the seven seas.

This book has four different endings so if you haven't seen them all, you can:

Go back one step and keep trying to get out of the quicksand without the help of Percival, Becky, and Pamela (turn to page 235).

Go back two steps and send Marina and McCartney to get the treasure instead of going yourself (turn to page 203).

Go back to the beginning and re-read the first scene (turn to page 193).

If you've read all four endings, turn to page 261.

You and Uncle Six are back in the quicksand and this time you're going to keep trying to get out without the help of Percival, Becky, and Pamela.

TRY TO GET OUT OF THE QUICKSAND ON YOUR OWN

You decide to keep trying to get out on your own. Dividing the treasure into eight shares instead of five means that you and each member of your crew will get a lot less treasure. For instance, if the treasure contains 800 gold coins and you divide it into five shares, you each get 160 coins, because 800 divided by five is 160. However, if you divide 800 coins into eight shares, you each only get 100 coins. It's just not worth it. You and Uncle Six are sure to get out of the quicksand, eventually. If you don't make it out on your own, your crew will come looking for you. The tricky trio doesn't have the treasure map, so they probably won't be able to find it on their own.

Percival, Becky, and Pamela walk in a wide circle around the quicksand and then keep going in the same direction you were headed before you fell in. They quickly disappear out of sight.

A couple hours later, you're still stuck and you regret your decision. Quicksand is uncomfortable! You and Uncle Six are both absolutely exhausted, and though you're unlikely to sink, it's probably a bad idea to fall asleep, even if you could. As evening approaches, you hear animal calls in the distance, and you get nervous. What if you're attacked by wild beasts? You won't be able to defend yourself.

You hear squelching footsteps heading toward you, and instead of calling for help, you and Uncle Six grow silent. It might be one of your crewmates, but what if it's an animal coming to eat you?

As the steps grow closer, you turn and look, terrified at what you might see.

It's just Becky. She's carrying a long rope.

"Still in there?" she says. "I thought you might be." She ties one end of the rope around a bush and throws you the other end.

You catch it and start trying to pull yourself from the quicksand.

"Gotta go," says Becky. "Papa's waiting in the ship for me."

"You're going?" you ask, surprised. You're surprised that they would leave without the treasure… Oh, no.

"Yep," she answers. "We found the treasure, no problem. We just walked in the same direction you'd been walking since you got on the island and we walked right into it. The chest wasn't even buried, just hidden under a few branches."

"But that's our treasure!" you say. With the help of the rope, you're slowly making progress at getting out. "That's not fair!"

"Sorry," she answers, "guess you should have taken the deal when we offered to pull you out of the quicksand. Then we'd only have three shares, instead of the whole thing."

"Will you take three shares now and give us the rest?" you ask.

"Sorry," she says, and scampers away.

"How about half?" you call after her.

She doesn't answer.

Once you and Uncle Six are out of the quicksand, you want to go after her, but Uncle Six waves you off.

"We're both exhausted," he says. "We'll never catch her, and besides, she came back and saved us from the quicksand. She didn't have to do that."

"But our treasure!" you say.

He just shakes his head, sadly. "That's the life of a pirate; sometimes you get the treasure, and sometimes someone else does. There'll be other maps and other treasures."

"But I need to find the treasure to prove to Grandpa Pirate that I'm ready to captain the Pickled Pearl. He'll never give me his infamous pirate ship, now!" you say.

"Maybe not," Uncle Six agrees.

The trip back to Pirate Town is somber. You love being at sea, but you're worried about how much sailing you'll be able to do in the future. Without the Pickled Pearl, will you have to get a job at the Pirate Town Farm? You like animals. There are worse jobs, you suppose, but your heart is at sea.

When you're finally back in Pirate Town, you sit in Grandpa Pirate's parlor.

"Well, my boy, you found the map, you got a sail, you provisioned the ship, and you got to the island, but you didn't get the treasure, and getting the treasure was the goal of the quest," says Grandpa Pirate.

"Yes, sir," you say, your head hanging.

"I don't think you're ready to captain such a large and infamous pirate ship as the Pickled Pearl," he says.

"No, sir," you say.

"But cheer up, my boy," he says. "You still have the Barnacle Bucket."

You look up. "I do?"

"You do," he answers. "She's a small ship, but a good one, and she's yours to captain until you're ready to take charge of the Pearl."

"Thank you, sir!" you exclaim.

"You're an able pirate, if a little inexperienced," he says. "You'll find other treasures and prove yourself worthy of the Pickled Pearl in time. I know you will."

"Thank you!" you say again.

Your decisions here had mixed results. You didn't get the treasure and win the Pickled Pearl, but your crew went on a quest and returned home safely. Dr. Fish got the quinine he needs to help lots of sick patients. You will continue to captain the Barnacle Bucket, and you still have the chance to prove yourself worthy of the Pickled Pearl.

This book has four different endings so if you haven't seen them all, you can:

Go back one step and ask Percival, Becky, and Pamela to pull you out of the quicksand (turn to page 226).
Go back two steps and send Marina and McCartney to get the treasure instead of going yourself (turn to page 203).
Go back to the beginning and re-read the first scene (turn to page 193).
If you've read all four endings, turn to page 261.

You're back on the Barnacle Bucket, and you've rescued Percival, Becky, and Pamela. This time you're going to ask Becky to help you find the way back to the island.

ASK BECKY TO NAVIGATE

The tricky trio has asked for three shares, and Dr. Fish has offered to give up his share if you take the deal. If you don't take the deal, you still have to pay his share, so the treasure will be divided into six shares if you don't accept Becky's offer to help, and eight shares if you do. Dividing the treasure into eight shares instead of six means that you and each member of your crew will get less treasure. For instance, if the treasure contains 48 gold coins and you divide it into six shares, you each get eight coins, because 48 divided by six is eight. However, if you divide 48 coins into eight shares, you each only get six coins. But you can't put a price on your friends' health and safety. What if it takes you a long time to find your way back to the island? What if you never find it? What if there are wild beasts or no fresh water? Mermaids are good at finding food in the ocean—shellfish, fish, and seaweed—but what if the island beaches don't have those things? Not all beaches are the same.

"All right," you tell Becky. "Take us back, and you each get a share of the treasure." You think it's pretty silly that the parrot gets a share, but their ship sank, so you can see why they need all the treasure they can get. You feel sorry for them.

Becky isn't able to complete her sextant measurements and navigational calculations until after local noon. When she does, you know you made the right choice asking for her help, because the storm blew you way off course. The island is nowhere near due east of your position. You would have been very lost without her.

As it is, you make it to the northern shore of the island a day later than you had planned. When you first spot the mermaids through the spyglass, you're very relieved. They're all right, and they have a chest with them! They swim out to the ship and leap onboard.

When McCartney sees Percival, Becky, and Pamela on deck, she grabs up a cutlass and looks about to attack.

"It's all right!" you tell her.

"What are these sneaky pirates doing here?" she asks.

You explain.

"We were so worried about you all," says Marina. "I'm so glad the Bucket's all right."

You nod and glance at Becky. She must feel awful that her ship sank.

She gives a small smile. "At least we have our lives," she says, "and three shares of treasure."

Opening the chest, you see it contains gold bars rather than coins. You won't be able to divide it until you can get back to Pirate Town and cut the bars into pieces.

Marina hands a sack to her father, Dr. Fish.

"What's this?" he asks and pulls some tree bark from the sack. His eyes widen. "Quinine!" he exclaims.

"What?" you ask.

"The treatment for deadly malaria," he says. "Where did you get this?"

"There was a cinchona tree on the island," Marina says. "I recognized it from the pictures you've shown me."

"That's wonderful!" Dr. Fish says. "This is more treasure than I could ever have hoped for."

"Good," says Percival, "because you gave up your share of the gold."

"Gold," Pamela echoes.

"And it was worth it," Dr. Fish says, and gives his daughter a hug.

The Barnacle Bucket sets sail for home.

That evening you have a celebration on board with extra rations. You ask the mermaids if they'll sing, but they're tired out from their adventure. You dance a jig for the ship's entertainment instead. Your audience is so moved by your performance that they weep… tears of laughter.

Your decisions worked out well. You've got the treasure, and you're headed home. You've completed Grandpa Pirate's quest, and you'll soon be captain of the Pickled Pearl, the best pirate ship in the seven seas.

This book has four different endings so if you haven't seen them all, you can:

Go back one step and try to find the island without Becky's help (turn to page 252).

Go back two steps and go find the treasure yourself instead of sending McCartney and Marina (turn to page 215).

Go back to the beginning and re-read the first scene (turn to page 193).

If you've read all four endings, turn to page 261.

You're back on the Barnacle Bucket, and you've rescued Percival, Becky, and Pamela. This time you're going to see if you can find the island without Becky's help.

FIND YOUR WAY BACK WITHOUT BECKY'S HELP

The tricky trio has asked for three shares, and Dr. Fish has offered to give up his share if you take the deal. If you don't take the deal, you still have to pay his share, so the treasure will be divided into six shares if you don't accept Becky's offer to help, and eight shares if you do. Dividing the treasure into eight shares instead of six means that you and each member of your crew will get a lot less treasure. For instance, if the treasure contains 480 gold coins and you divide it into six shares, you each get 80 coins, because 480 divided by six is 80. However, if you divide 480 coins into eight shares, you each only get 60 coins. It's just not worth it. You're worried about your friends, but mermaids are good at taking care of themselves. The map of the island shows plenty of (probably) fresh water, and they can find their own fish, shellfish, and seaweed in the ocean.

You turn the Barnacle Bucket due east and are confident that you'll find the island again within a day.

You don't.

Nor do you find it in three days.

Or four. Your crew tries to get you to reconsider taking the deal. Percival, Becky, and

Pamela won't budge. They won't accept less than three shares, and you refuse to pay that much. You've already looked for four days. Surely, you'll find the island soon.

On the fifth day, Uncle Wade, Uncle Six, and Dr. Fish offer their shares to the tricky trio for Becky's help finding the island. She does the sextant measurements and navigational calculations. The ship is much farther north than you thought. You sail southwest for three days and finally reach the island.

Looking through a spyglass, you don't see the mermaids on the northern shore. You take the rowboat to the island where you find a message written on a rock:

Dear Captain Patrick,

We hope you and the crew of the Barnacle Bucket are well. We know that the storm that hit the island likely also hit the ship. We're very worried about you.

We found the treasure and waited on the beach for a week. We ate the shellfish and seaweed we could find, but it wasn't much. The food on this beach isn't as plentiful as our cove in Pirate Town. We're very hungry. We saw a ship out at sea and signaled to it. We offered the pirates aboard the treasure in exchange for taking us back to Pirate Town. We hope to see you there.

Your friends,

McCartney and Marina.

The journey back to Pirate Town is terrible. The crew is mad at you for endangering Marina and McCartney, and the tricky trio is mad at you for losing the treasure.

When you finally make it back, you can't bear to face Grandpa Pirate. You know he'll never make you captain of the Pickled Pearl now. You hear that McCartney and Marina made it home safely, but you don't go to visit them at the mermaid cove. You're sure they blame you for abandoning them on the island. You get a job at Pirate Town Farm helping Aunt Farmer take care of the animals. You like it well enough. You like animals.

One day, you're mucking out the pigsty, when you hear someone walk up behind you. "Hello, my boy," says Grandpa Pirate.

"Hello, sir," you answer, your head bowed.

"My sister tells me you're doing good work caring for her animals," he says.

"Thank you, sir," you answer.

"I thought it was about time that I come see you," Grandpa Pirate says.

You don't answer.

"Do you want to be a farmer?" he asks. "Are you done with piracy?"

"I'm not cut out to be a pirate captain," you say. "I endangered Marina and McCartney, and I lost the treasure."

He sighs. "Well, I'll be honest, my boy. You made a huge mistake. You're clearly not ready to be a captain… yet, but you could be a part of a crew. You could follow orders instead of giving them. Maybe someday…"

"Maybe someday I'll be a captain?" you ask.

"Maybe," he answers. "Or you can stay here. My sister is getting older. Just like I'm getting ready to retire, so is she. She chose farming over piracy. You could make the same choice."

You nod. "I like animals," you say.

"I know," he says, "but do you still love

the sea?"

You sigh. "I do," you say.

"What do you want to do?" he asks.

"I don't know," you answer.

He pats your shoulder. "Well, you have plenty of time to decide. I'll see you around, my boy."

"See you," you say.

That night you go to see the mermaids. "I'm sorry I left you on the island," you tell them. "I thought I'd be able to find it without Becky's help."

McCartney just sniffs and turns away, but Marina takes your hand. "I forgive you," she says, and you know you're still friends.

Your choices turned out horribly. At least you like farming. You can still be a pirate if you want to, just not a captain, not for now, anyway.

This book has four different endings so if you haven't seen them all, you can:

Go back one step and ask for Becky's help to find the island (turn to page 244).
Go back two steps and go find the treasure yourself instead of sending McCartney and Marina (turn to page 215).
Go back to the beginning and re-read the first scene (turn to page 193).
If you've read all four endings, turn to page 261.

A LITTLE BOOK OF BIG CHOICES

MATH PIRATES

DIVIDING THE PLUNDER

BOOK 5: DIVISION & FRACTIONS

S.E. BURR

DIVIDING THE PLUNDER

The treasure you found using the map you got from Pirate Pete contains 55 gold bars. These bars need to be divided into eight equal shares—one for you, four for the members of your crew (except Dr. Fish who gave up his share), and three for Percival the Sneaky Pirate's crew. Percival's crew is made up of himself, his daughter Becky, and their Parrot

Pamela. You still think it's nuts that a parrot gets a share, but oh well, you made the deal. Now you have to abide by it.

In the hold of the Barnacle Bucket, anchored at the Pirate Town Dock, you divide the treasure. You give each person (and parrot) a bar of gold and keep one for yourself. You do this six times. You've given out 48 gold bars because six times eight is 48. Now you have seven bars left and you can't divide seven bars evenly between eight people.

"Bring down the jeweler," you say.

"Aye aye, captain!" says Uncle Six. He climbs the stairs up to the deck and returns a moment later with Jeremiah the Jeweler, who has been waiting patiently above.

"Jeremiah," you say. "I see you've brought your equipment. We need to you to divide six gold bars into pieces for us, so we all get even shares. You will get a gold bar as payment." You hand him the gold bar, and he puts it in his pocket.

"Now wait," says Percival the Pirate, "he gets an entire gold bar just for dividing up six bars?"

"Aye," you answer.

"Seems like a waste of gold to me," says Percival.

Jeremiah reddens. "Now, see here! My profession requires a long apprenticeship and precision tools! One gold bar is a bargain!"

Percival sniffs. "If you say so."

Jeremiah is about to respond, but you speak first. You look at Percival. "If you think we're paying too much to have the bars divided, there's a simple solution."

"What's that?" he asks.

"If you give up your gold bar, we can

divide the seven remaining bars between the rest of us, and we won't need Jeremiah's services."

Jeremiah splutters. "I came all the way over here and waited to help you with this. Now you don't want my services?"

You pat him on the shoulder and raise your eyebrows toward Percival. Jeremiah falls silent.

"No!" says Percival. "No, no, let the man do his work. That's fine."

"That's what I thought," you say with a smile.

Jeremiah takes a deep breath. "Now that that's settled, how do you want them divided?"

"Please start by dividing all six bars in half," you say.

Jeremiah cuts each gold bar into two equal pieces. The six gold bars become 12 half bars. You hand a half gold bar to each person (except Jeremiah.) That leaves four half bars (equal to two full bars.)

"Now what?" asks Jeremiah.

"Please divide the half bars in half again," you say.

So, Jeremiah cuts each half bar into two equal pieces. Each of the two gold bars are now divided into four quarters, for a total of eight quarter bars. You hand out the eight quarter bars. Now you're done dividing the plunder.

You thank Jeremiah, and Uncle Six leads him back up the stairs.

Each of you has received six and three-quarters gold bars (6 + 1/2 + 1/4.)

"What is everyone going to do with your share of the treasure?" you ask.

"I'm going to buy a more precise sextant," says McCartney. "It'll give my navigation maximum accuracy."

Marina says she's going to save her share for a rainy day.

Uncle Six says he's going to raise the roof on his house so he'll stop bumping his head.

Uncle Wade says he's in the market for some new waders.

"Gold!" squawks Pamela.

"No, ma'am," says Percival to the bird. He puts some shiny pieces of tin in front of her, which distracts her so he can take her share. "Hand yours over, too, Becky," he says to his daughter.

"Hey, that's not right," you say. "She earned that fair and square. You should let her keep it."

Becky smiles at you, but shrugs and hands her father her gold.

"What are you going to do with all that

gold anyway?" Uncle Six asks Percival.

Percival gives a dashing smile. "I'm finally going to achieve my dream," he says.

"Your dream?" you ask.

"I'm going to open a used ship dealership—great ships at great prices," he says. "Hey, why don't you trade in this old bucket for something more maneuverable? I can put you in a pretty little sloop. I'll give you a great bargain since we're friends."

"Friends?" you echo in disbelief. He tried to steal the treasure from you and then swindled his way into three shares. You're NOT friends.

Uncle Six pats your shoulder. "Finding the treasure was a quest set by Grandpa Pirate for Patrick to prove his piracy skills," he says. "Patrick here is the new captain of the Pickled Pearl."

"The P-P-Pickled Pearl?" Percival sputters.

Uncle Six chuckles. "So, you've heard of it."

"It's only the most fearsome pirate ship in all the seven seas," says Becky. "Let's go, dad," she says and then she, Percival, and Pamela leave.

"So, what are you going to do with your share of the treasure, Patrick?" Marina asks.

"Well, I have a couple ideas," you say, "but I probably only have enough gold to do one of them. I'll either buy an awesome new figurehead for the Pearl or I'll throw a party to celebrate achieving the quest. I thought that would be a good way to meet my new crew and say thank you to everyone that has helped me, the Crew of the Barnacle Bucket and some folks in town."

"A new figurehead would be nice," says McCartney. "You could get something terrifying like a sea serpent!"

"But a party would sure be fun," says Dr. Fish.

"Which are you going to do?" Marina asks.

Will you get a new figurehead (turn to page 280)?

Or

Will you throw a party (turn to page 273)?

You're back in the hold of the Barnacle Bucket, and this time you make a different choice. You decide to throw a party.

THROW A PARTY

Grandpa Pirate takes you on a tour of the Pickled Pearl to see the ship and meet her crew. You've already met the first mate, Pete. He's the one who gave you the map you used to find the treasure. Several of the other crew members you recognize as members of Pete's crochet circle. Apparently, crochet is a popular pastime upon the Pickled Pearl.

"A couple of my people have decided to leave the life of piracy and have taken positions in port," says Grandpa Pirate. "You'll need to find replacements for the ship's doctor and the navigator."

"Aye," you say, looking around in awe. The ship is just as beautiful and fearsome as you remember, though you haven't been aboard since you were a small child riding high as Grandpa Pirate carried you on his shoulders. She's a full-rigged frigate, speedy and agile for her large size. All she's missing is a fearsome figurehead, but that will have to wait. Now it's time to throw a party.

You decide the best place for the party is right here on the deck of the Pickled Pearl.

You ask some of the food stands in the square to cater. Eel stew and meat pies are two of the delicious foods they bring. Aunt Farmer provides fruit and veggie trays, goat cheese, and hard-boiled eggs. Yum! Tommo from Tommo's Tattoo Table is there to give anyone who wants one a free temporary tattoo. The owner of Sea Shanty Singalong is on deck to lead guests in some rousing singalongs. It's going to be a great party.

You invite your new crew, the crew of the Pickled Pearl. You also invite the crew of the Barnacle Bucket who helped you find the treasure. You even invite Percival, Becky, and Pamela. That tricky trio did everything they could to beat you to the treasure, but they helped you in the end. You invite the other people who helped you on your quest, like those who helped you find Pirate Pete, and those that gave you snacks or advice along the way. Finally, you invite all the mermaids at the cove. They've given you dinner more times than you can count, and they always invite you to their full moon dances.

The party is a great success. At the beginning of the evening, you run around making sure that everyone has enough to eat and drink and is having a good time. After a while, you settle down and enjoy yourself. You join in with a sea shanty about the old Derby Ram:

Now the night 'twas wet and
rough, sir, the wind was blowing
shrill.
He borrowed my suit of oilskins,
he took my trick at the wheel.
That's a lie, that's a lie, that's a lie,
lie, lie.
The pirates that are singing are
handsome, strong and brave,

The smartest bunch of sailers, and
always well-behaved.
That's the truth! That's the truth!
That's the truth, truth, truth!

Then there's a long pause and everyone starts to laugh, and then you all sing the real chorus.

That's a lie! That's a lie! That's a lie,
lie, lie!

After the singing, you go over to Tommo's Tattoo Table to get yourself a temporary tattoo. There are two you particularly like and you set the pictures side by side on the table to consider. One is a mermaid and one is a fish.

Do you choose the mermaid tattoo (turn to

page 289)?

Or

Do you choose the fish tattoo (turn to

page 298)?

You're back in the hold of the Barnacle Bucket, and this time you make a different choice. You decide to buy a figurehead.

BUY A FIGUREHEAD

Grandpa Pirate takes you on a tour of the Pickled Pearl to see the ship and meet her crew. You've already met some of them, including the first mate, Pete.

"A couple of my people have left the life of piracy and have taken positions in port," says Grandpa Pirate. "You'll need to find replacements for the ship's doctor and the navigator."

"Aye," you say, looking around in awe. The ship is just as beautiful and fearsome as you remember, though you haven't been aboard in a long time. She's a full-rigged frigate, speedy and agile for her large size.

All she's missing is a fearsome figurehead, and it's time to buy one. A party would be fun, and might be a good way to get to know your new crew a little better. However, a new figurehead is good luck for a new captain, and pirate crews really like feeling lucky.

You head to Fantastic Figureheads, the best place to buy figureheads in Pirate Town.

The proprietor of Fantastic Figureheads is named Sam. He has an eye patch on his left eye. His hair and beard are red, and he's wearing fashionable striped pants. He bears some resemblance to Pirate Pete, the first mate of the

Pickled Pearl. As you walk into the workshop, you see him carving a figurehead with a chisel.

"Are you carving a turtle?" you ask him.

"A tortoise," he answers. He steps to the side so you can get a better view. "See the feet. This beasty lives on the land, not in the sea."

"Why would anyone want to put a tortoise on the front of their ship?" you ask.

"Why not?" he asks.

You laugh. Isn't it obvious? "Like you just said, they live on the land, not in the sea."

He shrugs. "So do lions, and unicorns, and lots of other things people use for their figureheads."

"Unicorns don't live on land," you say.

"They don't?" he asks.

"Well, I suppose they do," you answer, "or they would if they were real, but they're not."

"They're not?" he asks. "Are you sure?"

"Yes," you answer, "well, I mean, I think so."

"You think so?" he repeats, "so you think they are real?"

"No," you say, getting flustered. "I think they're not real."

"I used to think that mermaids weren't real," he says.

"That's ridiculous!" you say.

"Aye," he answers, "because now I live in Pirate Town and I've met many mermaids, but back in the old country? I never met a mermaid there, not a one."

"Just because you haven't seen something yourself, doesn't mean it's not real," you say.

"Aye," he answers, "so then unicorns might be real, too."

"I don't think so," you say, "but I suppose it's possible. I've heard tell of stranger animals.

In the Southern Hemisphere I heard there's a brown furry animal with webbed feet and the bill of a duck, and strangest of all, it lays eggs. It's called a plate-y-puss, or something like that."

"No way," says Sam. "A unicorn is one thing, but that's just ridiculous."

You shrug. "Yeah, you're probably right."

He goes back to his carving.

"Tortoises are slow," you say. "I can see using it on a barge or a raft, but a pirate ship? It's a strange choice."

"Aye, they are slow," Sam answers, "but I don't think it's such a strange choice. With their thick shells, they're strong and well defended, and they live a long time, longer than we humans do. I think it's a sensible figurehead for a captain who values safety and longevity."

You eye the carving up and down. It looks slow and plodding. There's nothing about it that would inspire fear, or awe, or envy. "We'll just have to agree to disagree," you say.

He chuckles, "Fair enough. So, how can I help you, Patrick? Surely, you haven't come to chat about unicorns and tortoises."

"No," you say and stand up straighter. "I am the new captain of the Pickled Pearl, and I have come for a figurehead, one fit for the finest ship in all the seven seas."

Sam's eyes widen. "Well, congratulations, captain," he says.

"Thank you," you answer.

"So, do you know what kind of figurehead you want?" he asks.

"I know I don't want a tortoise," you say, "but besides that I'm not sure. I thought I'd look at your drawings and get some ideas."

"Go ahead," he says, "every figurehead I've ever carved is pictured on these walls."

"Great," you say. "I'll look now and tell you what I want."

"Take your time," he says. "Whatever you pick, I won't be able to carve it for at least a month."

"A month!" you exclaim.

"Art takes time," he says, "and I have several customers who have already put in orders. If you want something right away, I have some figureheads in the back that people ordered but never paid for. Take a look."

You nod and head to the back of the shop. There are five figureheads sitting on the floor back there. Three you know you're not interested in: Rabbits are fast, but easily frightened. Lions are fearsome, but too frequently used as figureheads. The same is true of unicorns, and besides, if you're going to put something on the front of your ship, you want to know for sure whether or not it's real. What if someone asks?

Two figureheads catch your attention and you debate with yourself which you prefer. The mermaid is beautiful, a true work of art. Sam carved her hair with such detail that it almost looks real. She looks fast, and smart, and fun. The parrot, on the other hand, looks fearsome with a sharp beak and cunning eyes. It reminds you of Pamela.

You walk back over to Sam. "I'll take that one," you say.

"Which one?" he asks, looking toward the back of the shop where you're pointing.

Do you choose the mermaid figurehead (turn to page 305)?

Or

Do you choose the parrot figurehead (turn to page 312)?

You're back at Tommo's Tattoo Table and this time you make a different choice. You pick the mermaid tattoo.

THE MERMAID TATTOO

You decide to get the mermaid tattoo.

"Excellent choice," Tommo tells you.

You sit on a stool in front of his table, and using a stencil, he traces the design onto the inside of your forearm and then paints it.

"How long will this last?" you ask him as he works.

He takes a big sniff. "Hmm, judging by

your smell, I'd say about two weeks."

"My smell?" you ask.

"Aye," he answers. "The less you wash, the longer it lasts."

You feel your face grow hot and know you're blushing. "I washed before the party," you say.

"Exactly," he answers, "which is why I said two weeks. Seems to me, you're a more frequent bather than many round these parts, though less frequent than some."

"What's the shortest amount of time one of your tattoos has lasted?" you ask him.

"Have you heard of the Pristine Prince?" he asks.

"The Pristine Pirate Prince? Aye," you say.

"He visited Pirate Town a couple years ago, and he asked me to give him a temporary tattoo of a whiskey bottle," Tommo says.

"A whiskey bottle?" you repeat. You'd never heard that the Pristine Prince was a drinker.

"Aye," Tommo says. "I think because whiskey is good for cleaning wounds and such."

"Oh, aye," you say.

He goes on. "No sooner had I started tracing the design than he said 'stop,' and told me to wash it off quick before it dried."

"Strange," you say. "He changed his mind before you even finished putting it on?"

"Aye. He said the paint felt too dirty on his skin," says Tommo.

"I reckon he's a real stickler for cleanliness," you say.

"I reckon so," says Tommo, "but I'll tell you what a big part of his trouble was and what might have scared him away. Melly the Smelly had come up behind him and was looking over his shoulder at my work."

"Oh," you say.

"Oh is right," he answers. "Melly has an awful powerful odor, and the prince strikes me as one with an awful sensitive nose."

"I'll bet," you say.

"Anyway, it all worked out in the end because Melly asked me to give her a temporary tattoo of a skunk," he says.

"A skunk?" you ask. "Do you have a stencil for that?"

He laughs. "No. It's not exactly a popular request, although it is a formidable animal. I did it freehand, and I was mighty proud of how it turned out. It's still on Melly's arm today, as she is not one to wash."

"Wow," is all you can say.

He finishes up the tattoo. "What do you

think?" he asks.

You examine his handiwork. "It looks great!" you exclaim. Besides being beautiful, the mermaid looks tough, like she would win in a fistfight with a shark. She also looks friendly, like she would offer you eel stew or ask you to dance at one of the full moon dances at Mermaid Cove.

"Thanks, Tommo!"

"You're very welcome, captain," he answers.

You stand and let the next person in line take your place. As you walk away, your friend Marina and her parents approach you.

"Hello Patrick!" she says. "Great party."

"Hello, Marina," you answer. "Hello Dr. Fish and Dr. Fish."

There are two doctors in Marina's family. One Dr. Fish is a mermaid, and she's Marina's mom. The other Dr. Fish is a man, he's Marina's dad, and he accompanied you on your treasure hunt. He ended up giving up his share of the treasure, but found quinine, a treatment for malaria, which he said was treasure enough for him.

Dr. Fish, Marina's mom, is eating a hard-boiled egg. "Great food!" she says.

"Thanks," you answer.

Dr. Fish, Marina's dad, says, "What kind of temporary tattoo did you get?"

You hold out your arm for them to see.

"A mermaid?" asks Dr. Fish, Marina's mom. "Well, isn't that interesting?"

"I like it a lot," says Marina's dad, and gives his wife a small smile. "She looks a bit like you, though not as beautiful and fierce."

She smiles back.

Marina's dad says, "We heard you're

looking for a doctor for your next voyage?"

"Aye, sir," you answer.

"I volunteer," he says. "Marina and I enjoyed sailing with you on your last voyage, and we would be happy to accompany you on the next one."

"Yeah, we would!" says Marina.

"I would be glad to have you!" you answer.

Your choices worked out well. You threw a splendid party. You found a ship's doctor for your next voyage. Your best friend, Marina, is planning to come, too. You still need to find a navigator, but you're confident that you'll be able to find one before it's time to set sail on your next adventure.

This book has four endings so if you haven't seen them all you can:

Go back one step and get the fish tattoo (turn to page 297).

Go back two steps and buy a figurehead (turn to page 279).

Go back to the beginning and re-read the first scene (turn to page 263).

If you've read all four endings, then turn to page 318.

You're back at Tommo's Tattoo Table and this time you make a different choice. You pick the fish tattoo.

THE FISH TATTOO

You decide to get the fish tattoo. "Excellent choice," Tommo tells you. You sit on a stool in front of his table, and using a stencil, he traces the design onto the inside of your forearm and then paints it.

"How long will this last?" you ask him as he works.

He takes a big sniff. "Hmm, judging by your smell, I'd say about two weeks."

"My smell?" you ask.

"Aye," he answers. "The less you wash, the longer in lasts."

You feel your face grow hot and know you're blushing. "I washed before the party," you say.

"Exactly," he answers, "which is why I said two weeks. Seems to me, you're a more frequent bather than many round these parts."

"What's the longest one of your temporary tattoos has ever lasted?" you ask.

"You know the pirate lass, Melly the Smelly?" he asks.

"Aye," you answer.

"I gave her a skunk tattoo over two years ago and she's still got it," he says.

"Wow," you say. "Doesn't sound very

temporary."

He shakes his head. "Nigh unto permanent since she never bathes," he answers.

He finishes the design, and you examine his handiwork. It looks great! The fish looks big and tough, like it would win in a fight with a shark, but also friendly like it wouldn't mind being in a school. A school of fish, that is. It would be hard to fit this behemoth in a classroom fishbowl.

"Thanks, Tommo!" you exclaim.

"You're very welcome, captain," he answers.

You stand and let the next person in line take your place. As you walk away, your friend Marina and her parents approach you.

"Hello Patrick!" she says. "Great party."

"Hello, Marina," you answer. "Hello Dr. Fish and Dr. Fish."

There are two doctors in Marina's family. One Dr. Fish is a mermaid, and she's Marina's mom. The other Dr. Fish is a man, he's Marina's dad, and he accompanied you on your treasure hunt. He ended up giving up his share of the treasure, but found quinine, a treatment for malaria, which he said was treasure enough for him.

Dr. Fish, Marina's dad, is chewing on a carrot. "I love the veggie trays!" he says. "Aunt Farmer grows some tasty vegetables."

"She sure does," you agree.

Dr. Fish, Marina's mom, says, "Did you just get a temporary tattoo? Can we see it?"

You hold out your arm for them to see.

"A fish?" asks Dr. Fish, Marina's dad. "Well, isn't that interesting?"

"I like it a lot," says Marina's mom. "There's nothing I like much more than a good-looking fish." She gives her husband a small smile.

He smiles back.

Marina's mom says, "We heard you're looking for a doctor for your next voyage?"

"Aye, ma'am," you answer.

"I volunteer," she says. "Marina and I would love to sail on your next voyage."

"Yeah, we would!" says Marina.

"I would be glad to have you!" you answer.

Your choices worked out well. You threw a splendid party. You found a ship's doctor for your next voyage. Your best friend, Marina, is planning to come too. You still need to find a navigator, but you're confident that you'll be able to find one before it's time to set sail on your next adventure.

This book has four endings so if you haven't seen them all you can:

Go back one step and get the mermaid tattoo (turn to page 288).

Go back two steps and buy a figurehead (turn to page 279).

Go back to the beginning and re-read the first scene (turn to page 263).

If you've read all four endings, then turn to page 318.

You're back at Fantastic Figureheads and this time you make a different choice. You pick the mermaid figurehead.

THE MERMAID FIGUREHEAD

You decide to get the mermaid figurehead. You borrow Aunt Farmer's cart and horse to transport it to the docks.

At the Pickled Pearl, the few crewmen on deck give a cheer when they see it. A new figurehead for a new captain is considered a lucky thing, and pirates like to feel lucky.

"What will we call her?" Pirate Pete, the first mate, asks.

You pause, furrowing your brow. "Sam didn't tell me whether the mermaid has a name," you say.

At that moment, a mermaid leaps onto the deck. It's McCartney, your cousin, who had been your navigator on the voyage to find the treasure. "Hello Patrick," she says, nodding to you.

"Hello McCartney, welcome aboard the Pearl," you answer.

"Thanks," she says. She nods to the first mate. "Hello Pete."

"Hello Miss McCartney," he answers.

"Hello Grandmother Melusine," she says, nodding to the figurehead.

You watch carefully to see if the statue will nod back. Of course, it doesn't.

"Grandmother Melusine?" you ask. The figurehead is of a young merson, a mer-person, not old enough to be anyone's grandmother.

"Aye," McCartney answers. "Surely, it's a carving of Melusine, first of the mermaids and grandmother to all the mer-people who came after. She was human once but her mother changed her into a mermaid."

"Why?" you ask.

"As a punishment according to the human tales," she says, "but we mermaids know it was really a gift. It's much more fun to be a merson than a person."

You laugh. "We'll have to agree to disagree," you say. "I know you love living in the water, but I love sailing on top of it. A pirate is what I'm meant to be."

"A merson can be both a mermaid and a pirate," she says.

"Of course," you answer, "but you never really feel at home on ship, do you? That's why you sleep in the water."

"Aye, true," she says. "Sailing is not nearly so nice as swimming. Even so, I'm here to volunteer for another voyage."

"You are?" you ask. "That's great! We need a navigator."

"I heard," says McCartney. "And I'm ready to go on another adventure and win some more treasure."

McCartney touches the carving's hair. "It's a beautiful figurehead," she says.

"Thank you," you answer.

"Some legends of Melusine say she was turned part dragon, rather than part fish," she says.

"That can't be true, can it?" asks Pete. "Not if you're descended from her."

McCartney looks down at her tail. "Aye, it looks like a fish's tail, but maybe it's actually the tail of a dragon," she says. "Do you know what a dragon's tail looks like?"

"Nay," says Pete, and you shake your head.

"Me neither," McCartney says wistfully, but then she smiles. "But one thing I know about dragons is that they love treasure, so when do we sail?"

Your choices worked out well. You got a beautiful and lucky figurehead quickly and at a fair price. You found a navigator for your next voyage. You still need a ship's doctor, but you're confident that you'll be able to find one before it's time to set sail on your next adventure.

This book has four endings so if you haven't seen them all you can:

Go back one step and get the parrot figurehead (turn to page 311).

Go back two steps and throw a party (turn to page 272).

Go back to the beginning and re-read the first scene (turn to page 263).

If you've read all four endings, then turn to page 318.

You're back at Fantastic Figureheads, and this time you make a different choice. You pick the parrot figurehead.

THE PARROT FIGUREHEAD

You decide to get the parrot figurehead. You borrow Aunt Farmer's cart and horse to transport it to the docks.

As you're driving away from Fantastic Figureheads, you see a familiar flash of red feathers out of the corner of your eye, and then you look back to see a Parrot swoop down and land on the parrot figurehead in the wagon.

You stop the wagon. "Hello, Pamela," you say to the bird.

She ignores you.

A moment later, Becky hops up onto the wagon seat beside you. "Hi Patrick," she says.

"Hi Becky," you answer.

You click your tongue, and the horse starts walking again.

"Pamela and I really like your figurehead," she says.

You laugh. "I'm not surprised. It looks an awful lot like Pamela."

Becky looks at the figurehead and back at you. "That it does...Why did you choose that figurehead?" she asks.

You shrug. "Someone ordered it but didn't pay for it, so I got a discount and could pick it up right away."

"Oh," she says, and she sounds a little

sad.

Something occurs to you. "Was your dad the one who ordered the parrot figurehead and didn't pay for it?" you ask.

She laughs. "No!"

"Are you sure?" you ask.

"Yes," she says. "It wasn't us."

In that case, what's bothering her? you wonder.

"It wasn't my only choice," you say. "There were other figureheads that people had ordered but not paid for, too."

She smiles at that. "Oh really?" she asks.

"Really," you answer.

"So, why did you pick the parrot?" she asks.

You shrug. "I just like it, I guess."

"But why do you like it?" she asks.

Her questions are getting a little irritating,

but you take a deep breath and answer.

"It seems fierce and clever. You see the parrot and you immediately think 'Pirate.' It seems like an excellent symbol for a pirate ship," you say.

"I agree," says Becky. "Pamela is very piratical."

"I wasn't talking about Pamela," you say.

"But the figurehead looks just like her," she says, "and Pamela was born to be a pirate. So was I."

"I thought you were going into the used boat business," you say.

"That's my father's dream," she says. "Not ours. Our hearts are at sea, and we're eager to set sail again. We heard you're looking for a couple of crew members."

You give a sharp laugh. "Oh, no! I'm not falling for that again. Pamela is a pet, not a crew member, and she's not getting any more shares of treasure."

"Gold!" says Pamela.

"Sorry, Pam," says Becky, "guess you'll have to share my share of the treasure."

"Gold!" the bird says again.

Becky looks at you. "It was worth a try. Fine, one share of future plunder for me and Pamela together. Do we have a deal?"

You think for a minute. Becky and Pamela are an awfully tricky duo, but they're fine pirates, and you need a navigator. "Deal," you say, as you stop the cart on the dock near your ship. "Welcome aboard the Pickled Pearl."

Your choices worked out well. You got a fierce and lucky figurehead quickly and at a fair price. You found a navigator for your next voyage. You still need a ship's doctor, but you're confident that you'll be able to find one before it's time to set sail on your next adventure.

This book has four endings so if you haven't seen them all you can:

Go back one step and get the mermaid figurehead (turn to page 304).

Go back two steps and throw a party (turn to page 272).

Go back to the beginning and re-read the first scene (turn to page 263).

If you've read all four endings, then turn to page 318.

CONGRATULATIONS!

Y ou've completed the final task in your quest for the Pickled Pearl! Congratulations, Captain.

GET FREE BOOKS!

When you sign up for our mailing list at littlebooksofBIGchoices.com, you will receive the first book of every series we write for free. Head on over and sign up today!

littlebooksofBIGchoices.com

ABOUT THE AUTHOR

Once upon a time there were two little girls named Margaret.

One of the Margarets had brown hair and the other had red, and they were both poor and lived on farms, because in those days most little girls were poor and lived on farms.

And when the Margarets got older, they went to college, even though poor girls rarely did, but the Margarets were stubborn and lucky, so they got to go.

Brown-Haired Margaret became a nurse and then a librarian. Red-Haired-Margaret became a school teacher. They spent their lives helping, teaching, and reading.

Who did they help, teach, and read to the most?

Their children, of course.

Brown-Haired-Margaret had a son and Red-Haired-Margaret had a daughter, and that son and that daughter met and fell in love, and together they spent their lives reading, which is almost a happy ending...

But not quite, because what made the story even better, was that the son and the daughter had a daughter of their own and they raised her in libraries and in bookstores and left her to her own devices to play and to wander among the stacks of books, where she found innumerable adventures waiting for her between the pages.

The brown-haired Margaret and the red-haired Margaret both became white-haired-Margarets and they continued to help, and teach, and read.

And who did they help, teach, and read

to the most?

Their granddaughter, of course!

She grew up to love books EVEN MORE, than her parents had. She loved books so much, in fact, that she wanted to make more of them, and because she was stubborn and lucky, she did.

S.E. Burr's greatest desire is to spend her life helping, teaching, and reading like her grandmothers did.